THE
CRAPPIE
FISHING
HANDBOOK

PHOTO BY Penny Berryman

THE

CRAPPIE
FISHING
HANDBOOK

Tackle, Lures, Bait, Cooking, Tips,
Tactics and Techniques

KEITH SUTTON

Skyhorse Publishing

Skyhorse Publishing books may be purchased in bulk at special discounts for sales promotion, corporate gifts, fund-raising, or educational purposes. Special editions can also be created to specifications. For details, contact the Special Sales Department, Skyhorse Publishing, 307 West 36th Street, 11th Floor, New York, NY 10018 or info@skyhorsepublishing.com.

Skyhorse® and Skyhorse Publishing® are registered trademarks of Skyhorse Publishing, Inc.®, a Delaware corporation.

Visit our website at www.skyhorsepublishing.com.
10 9 8 7 6 5 4 3

Library of Congress Cataloging-in-Publication Data is available on file.

ISBN: 978-1-61608-540-7

Printed in China

To Big Josh, Little Josh, Matt, Shaun, Jared and Zach. No father has ever been more proud of his sons' accomplishments, more blessed with familial friendships or so fortunate to have shared so many treasured moments in God's great outdoors.

CONTENTS

Section VI: TACTICAL TIPS

Section VII: TROPHY TACTICS

Section VIII: CLEANING AND COOKING CRAPPIE

FOREWORD

Look up "crappie" in the dictionary, and you won't see a picture of Keith Sutton there. That's a mistake on the part of Messrs. Funk and Wagnall. I've been in this outdoor writing business for . . . well, let's just say a long time. And in all those years, I've never run across anybody who knows more about crappie, and about catching them, than the guy whose name is on the cover of this book.

I've known this Sutton character most of those many years because he's been in this same business for about as long as I have. Our career paths have crossed and recrossed since the 1970s when we were both struggling freelancers trying with mixed success to break into the outdoor-magazine business. We were friends and competitors back then, and when we were both hired by the same state natural resources agency in the early 1980s, it added another layer to our relationship; we became not only friends and competitors, but also co-workers.

For nearly twenty years, among other numerous duties, we worked on the agency's award-winning magazine—Keith as editor, me as his able-bodied assistant—and we turned out a product that, if you don't mind me saying so, was consistently excellent and sometimes downright brilliant. Throughout those two decades, we pushed each other to be better writers and photographers, each of us editing and critiquing the other's stuff, brainstorming the magazine's content, arguing (sometimes heatedly) over ideas, wording, magazine content and layout and just about everything else you can think of. But evidently all that arguing and pushing each other worked, because the magazine and our individual work in it earned scores of awards from the Association for Conservation Information, the Outdoor Writers Association of America and the Southeastern Outdoor Press Association. One issue earned Sutton and me joint recognition as Conservation Communicators of the Year from the Arkansas Wildlife Federation.

I tell you these things not to brag—well, maybe a little—but to give you some idea why I'm qualified to talk about the guy whose book you're now holding. Through all those years, when Sutton and I weren't working on the magazine and other agency projects, we boondocked around the wilder parts of the world—duck hunting, squirrel hunting, bass fishing, bream fishing and, yes, crappie fishing. And if I ever came close to holding up my end of the boat when Keith Sutton was in the other end of it, I don't remember it. The man is a crappie-catching machine. He thinks like a crappie, or at least I assume he does, because he can catch them when lesser mortals like me can't buy a bite. If I had one minnow (or one jig or whatever) and I needed a crappie to save my life, Sutton is the guy I'd give it to. He's that good.

This crappie machine is also a world-class outdoor communicator, as evidenced by all those writing and photography awards I mentioned. He's one of the best in this business, with a reputation that spans not only the country but the globe. When he finishes a magazine story or newspaper column, or a book like this one, you can rest assured it's the best he can possibly make it. In case you don't yet get what I'm driving at, that's pretty darn good.

So what you have in this book is the melding of two passions: outdoor communications and crappie fishing. Keith Sutton is among the best in the world at both, and just as he and I used to push each other to be better, the combination of these two things has produced a book that's second to none. Pay attention to the stuff in these pages, and it will make you a better crappie angler. Pay attention to how that stuff is presented, and it will make you a better writer as well.

—**Jim Spencer**
www.treblehookunlimited.com

INTRODUCTION

Many books have been written about crappie fishing. I'm a fan of all I have read, and to be honest, the folks who wrote those books—people like Steve Wunderle, Tim Huffman, Jim Robbins, Larry Larsen, Horace Carter, Bill Dance and Charlie Brewer—know more about crappie fishing than I'll ever learn.

That being the case, you might wonder why I've written yet another treatise about fishing for America's favorite panfish.

First of all, this book is a labor of love. I enjoy fishing for all kinds of fish. Crappie, however, rank near the top on my favorites list. I started fishing for them at age six and immediately fell in love with these calico sunfish. That love never diminished. Put me on a backcountry crappie lake with a cane pole and a few minnows and jigs, and I'm as happy as a man can be. Being a writer, it's only natural I should want to share my thoughts about something I enjoy so much.

Second, I believe I have unique insights on the sport worth sharing. You'll find lots of basic information on these pages, for sure. You'll learn about crappie biology, the types of structure and cover to fish, how to select and use basic crappie-catchers

PHOTO BY **Owen Blake**

such as jigs and minnows and tried-and-true tactics for catching crappie throughout the seasons. But you'll also discover many new and innovative ways of finding and catching crappie. I've been fortunate to fish with some of the country's finest crappie anglers, and more fortunate still that they've been willing to share much of their knowledge. You'll find their insights transformed into text on the pages inside. I've also spent a lifetime studying crappie behavior in the lakes and rivers I fish, and the things I've discovered firsthand provide the basis for much of the information here.

Finally, I think it's time someone gave crappie anglers a book they can be proud to lay on their coffee tables for others to see, a book that's more than just black-and-white text and photos. My publisher feels the same way. Crappie are beautiful fish. Crappie fishing is a beautiful sport. This beauty should be shared in color photographs that entice others to try our sport, while at the same time providing worthwhile instruction and information that can help die-hard crappie fans be even better anglers.

I hope you enjoy this labor of love. I hope you learn many new things as you delve into the pages that follow. Most of all, I hope all your crappie-fishing adventures are fruitful and create memories that last a lifetime.

—**Keith Sutton**

Understanding Crappie

CRAPPIE BASICS

Its strike is often so delicate, it may be hooked before you know it. Seldom will one weighing much over a pound or two be caught. It puts up an admirable tussle on light tackle, but it's not really a hard fighter. So why is the crappie such a popular gamefish?

There's no single answer. Anglers laud the crappie for a combination of characteristics that make crappie fishing pure fun.

Crappie are found in thousands of lakes and streams through the U.S. In-the-know anglers haul them in spring, summer, autumn and winter. Anything these sunfish lack in size, they compensate for with sheer numbers and the ease with which they are caught.

Fancy equipment? No need. It doesn't matter if you use a homemade cane pole or a $200 ultralight rig. Both catch crappie.

Good eating? Absolutely. Crappie have flaky, white meat suitable for a variety of recipes. Nothing is tastier than crappie fillets properly prepared and cooked.

Crappie are fish for people of all ages. Sure, trout are bedazzling jumpers. Catfish are superb dinner fare. Stripers are brutal battlers. For many anglers, however, crappie are favorites because the certainty of some kind of fishing action is far better than promised battles that never come.

The Difference Between Black and White

The world has only two species of crappie—the black crappie (*Pomoxis nigromaculatus*) and the white crappie (*Pomoxis annularis*), both found exclusively in North America. They belong to the sunfish family, Centrarchidae, which also includes largemouth bass, bluegills and other popular warm-water gamefish.

Anglers seldom bother to distinguish between black crappie and white crappie. Both are uniquely beautiful panfish with large, showy fins and metallic

Crappie rank high among America's favorite sportfish. According to the 2006 National Survey of Fishing, Hunting and Wildlife-Associated Recreation (U.S. Fish and Wildlife Service), 6.21 million U.S. anglers over age 16 fish for them each year.

The differences between a white crappie (top) and black crappie (bottom) are minor, but most avid crappie anglers can readily distinguish one species from the other.

bodies that glisten like silver ingots. Fishing techniques are identical for each. Neither is more worthy quarry than the other, but if you catch a crappie big enough for the record books, it must be positively identified as one or the other.

The most reliable method of separating the two is counting the dorsal-fin spines. Black crappie normally have seven or eight; whites usually have six, but sometimes five.

Color is not as dependable, but white crappie are paler, and dark spots on the sides usually are arranged in regular vertical bars. Black crappie are typically darker and have scattered spots.

Black crappie fare best over a firm bottom in relatively cool, clear water. They strongly relate to aquatic vegetation. They're slightly fussier about their environment than white crappie, which flourish in warmer, siltier waters that often have soft substrates.

Some lakes and streams have populations of only one species. Over a great portion of their respective ranges, however, black crappie and white crappie live together in the same waters.

Most sage crappie anglers couldn't care less one way or the other. They're after crappie, plain and simple. And the type of crappie caught doesn't matter one iota.

Range

Black crappie originally were found in the eastern half of the United States except for the northeastern seaboard. The range of this species was greatly expanded, however, by introductions into eastern sections of the country where it wasn't found originally, and throughout the much of the West and the Midwest. Washington received its first stockings in 1890, California in 1891, Idaho in 1892 and Oregon in 1893.

The original range of the white crappie extended from eastern South Dakota to New York south to Alabama and Texas. This species also has been widely introduced into new waters, and like the black crappie, it now is found in all lower forty-eight states. It tends to be more at home in the oxbows, large lakes and sluggish rivers of the South, while the black crappie, which thrives best in colder, clearer water, ranges as far north as southern Canada.

Crappie also have been stocked in Mexico and Panama, with populations thriving in both countries.

Size

Average size depends on local conditions. One-half- to 1-pound crappie comprise most of the catch in most waters, but prime lakes and rivers often yield "barn doors" in the 2- to 3-pound class. Crappie weighing more than 3 pounds are very uncommon.

Black crappie growth generally is slower than that of the white crappie, but because it has a stockier body, a black crappie of a given length generally will weigh more than a white crappie of the same length. For example, a 12-inch black crappie will be heavier than a 12-inch white crappie.

The two primary record-keeping organizations—the International Game Fish Association and the National Fresh Water Fishing Hall of Fame—both recognize a 5-pound, 3-ounce white crappie caught in Enid Lake, Mississippi in 1957 as the all-tackle world record. However, the organizations differ in their listings when it comes to black crappie. The IGFA lists a black crappie weighing 5.0 pounds caught in a private pond in Callaway County, Missouri in 2006. The Hall of Fame's top white crappie is an even 6-pounder taken from Westwego Canal, Louisiana (a Mississippi River backwater) in 1969.

> **Did You Know?**
>
> In 1993, Louisiana became the first and only state to designate the crappie (in this case, the white crappie) as its official state fish.

In this Missouri Department of Conservation photo, John Horstman of Fulton, Missouri, poses with his 5-pound, 19-inch-long, world-record black crappie, caught in a Missouri pond on April 21, 2006.

This photo from the International Game Fish Association is one of few in existence showing Fred Bright of Memphis, Tennessee, with the 5-pound, 3-ounce, Enid Dam, Mississippi, white crappie that earned him a place in the world record books on July 31, 1957.

The Hall of Fame also lists an all-tackle record for the hybrid crappie, a cross between a black crappie and white crappie. That 2-pound, 11-ounce specimen was caught in Shabbona Lake, Illinois, in 2005. Although it's not listed as a world record, a 4-pound, 11-ounce hybrid crappie (21.5 inches long) caught from a Christian County watershed lake in May 2005 is the official Kentucky crappie record.

Food Habits

Crappie feed primarily on small fishes, aquatic insects and tiny crustaceans. The proportions of these food items vary with locality, season and the crappie's age. Young crappie feed more on small crustaceans. Adults subsist mainly on fish, with insects also making up a small percentage of the diet. Small shad are the principle food item for adult crappie in many reservoirs.

Biologists studying crappie in Arkansas' Beaver Lake found that adult black crappie tend to eat more insects in spring and fishes in other seasons, while adult white crappie eat fishes year-round. The researchers believe these food habits eventually caused white crappie to become more abundant in the reservoir than the previously dominant black crappie. As the lake aged, there was an apparent reduction in the number of insects important to black crappie, so the numbers of black crappie fell, and white crappie became the dominant species.

Reproduction

The fact that black crappie and white crappie select different spawning habitats is part of the reason they remain two distinct species. In some man-made lakes, however, the two crappie species sometimes overlap in their habitat, and they hybridize. The hybrids are sometimes called "gray crappie." And they may be more abundant in some waters than many people suspect. A study on Alabama's Weiss Lake, for example, determined that 18 percent of the population was hybrids and another 3 percent was offspring from hybrid parents.

Crappie move to shallows to nest in spring when the water temperature nears 56 degrees. That might be January in Florida and July in northern Ohio.

Adult males of both species undergo a noticeable color change as the season begins. Their cheeks and belly become considerably darker, and the upper sides often take on a brassy hue.

Males build the nests, using their tails to fan silt away from a bottom area composed of fine gravel or finely divided

Did You Know?

Several places lay claim to the title "Crappie Capital of the World," including Weiss Lake, Alabama; Kentucky Lake in Kentucky and Tennessee; Grand Lake, Oklahoma; and Lake Okeechobee, Florida.

WHAT'S IN A NAME?

The word *crappie* has its roots in the Canadian-French word *crapet*, which was an early name for the species. *Crapet* probably is derived from the French *crêpe*, a pancake, in reference to the fish's general shape.

In some areas, the name *crappie* has taken on a most indelicate pronunciation, similar to the dice game *craps*. Most people, however, pronounce it *croppie*, which is more in keeping with the word's derivation.

For many years, fish reference books referred to the white crappie simply as *crappie*, and the black crappie was known as the *calico bass*.

Crappie have more aliases than a most-wanted criminal, over fifty in all. Among the most commonly heard today are speck, speckled perch, white perch, calico, papermouth (in reference to the crappie's delicate mouth parts) and sac-a-lait (Cajun-French for "bag of milk"). More archaic nicknames include gold ring (for the iris of the eye), bachelor perch, banklick, chinquapin, lamplight, tinmouth, strawberry bass, silver perch, barfish, bridge perch, John Demon, timber crappie, Mason perch, straw bass, bitterhead, goggle-eye, shad, grass bass, Newlight and Campbellite.

The latter name, Campbellite, was mentioned in an 1878 biennial report by the Kansas State Board of Agriculture, which said, "[The crappie's] slang name in the West used to be the 'Campbellite,' because it made its first appearance in the tributaries of the Ohio about the time Alexander Campbell first began to achieve a reputation." Campbell was a religious leader of the early 1820s whose followers performed full-immersion baptisms and sometimes were referred to as Campbellites, New Light Christians or simply New Lights, the latter being another strange vernacular name associated with the crappie.

To avoid confusion caused by such a plethora of common names, scientific names are used. The black crappie's is *Pomoxis nigromaculatus*; the white crappie's is *Pomoxis annularis*. *Pomoxis* means sharp opercle, referring to the spiny, pointed rear edge of the gill cover. *Nigromaculatus* is Latin for "black spotted." *Annularis* is Latin for "having rings," a reference to the dark vertical bands on the white crappie's sides.

plant roots, often near a log or other large object. The nests almost invariably are in shallow coves protected from wave action, and there may be many nests in a single cove. The depth at which nests are found can vary considerably, from less than 1 foot to as much as 20 feet.

A large female crappie may lay as many as 180,000 eggs. Spawning with several males is common, and each female may produce eggs several times during the spawning period.

The eggs hatch in two to four days. The fry remain in the nest several days where they are guarded by the male.

When crappie reach the second or third summer of life, they are sexually mature and will spawn the following spring. The maximum life span is about seven or eight years, although few crappie live beyond age three or four.

Seasonal Behavior

Understanding the general seasonal habits of crappie is important so you can locate prime crappie-fishing areas year-round.

BLACKNOSE CRAPPIE

In many waters, anglers catch crappie that have a dark brown or black stripe running under the chin, over the nose and across part of the back. These beautifully marked fish, often considered special prizes by crappie fans, are called "blacknose crappie."

Several stories have been propagated to explain the origins of these fish. Most folks believe they are hybrid fish, a cross between black crappie and white crappie. Others believe they are juvenile crappie that lose the black stripe with age.

In fact, blacknose crappie are simply an unusual color strain of the black crappie. They were first described in Ohio in 1957. A later study reported they had been found in thirteen states. One of those states was Arkansas, where blacknose crappie turned up in Beaver and Bull Shoals lakes. Some of those fish were transported to an Arkansas state fish hatchery in the 1960s, where biologists learned how to propagate the strain and produce blacknose crappie by design rather than accident. This distinctive crappie is now being raised in hatcheries for stocking public fishing waters throughout the country. Because the blacknose is easily recognized even by untrained observers, it has proven valuable for studying crappie management strategies in lakes where it has been introduced.

Summer and winter crappie typically form large, loose schools and usually hold near cover in 10 to 35 feet of water. In oxbows, look for fish near old river channels or the basin of the lake. Reservoir fish may concentrate in deep timber near channel breaks or humps. River crappie tend to hole up in deep backwaters. Using a sonar fish finder makes the difficult job of locating these fish much simpler.

In spring, as the water temperature climbs into the upper 50s and low 60s, crappie move to their spawning grounds, usually in shallow, wind-protected coves with good cover. Most anglers find crappie near shoreline cover: willows, cypress trees, blowdowns, stick-ups and weed-beds. Larger crappie may be farther out over shallow, main-lake humps or near channel edges adjacent shallow flats.

Black crappie

White crappie

During cold fronts, crappie may leave shallows for deeper water. Deep timber along channel edges or underwater humps is a favorite retreat. The more severe the front, the deeper the fish withdraw.

Locating autumn crappie is especially hard. Fish in 8-foot depths one day may move to 20 feet the next. They may hold over brush piles in the morning and move to deep points by evening. The best advice this season is keep moving until you find feeding fish.

ART BY Duane Raver,
U.S. Fish and Wildlife Service

TWELVE PLACES YOU'LL ALWAYS FIND CRAPPIE

Lakes and rivers contain many crappie hotspots. If you're lucky, you can pick a spot at random, cast your bait and start reeling in slabs. But most of us aren't so lucky. For consistent success, especially on unfamiliar waters, we need more information; we need to know where, specifically, hungry crappie are likely to be.

Some places definitely are better than others, including the following twelve places where crappie gather like kids around an ice cream truck, gobbling every morsel that passes by.

Points

Points are excellent crappie hotspots year-round because they serve as pathways for fish moving back and forth between shallow and deep water. By working a point methodically from near-shore to offshore, you should be able to determine the day's depth pattern and use it to find crappie on other points or structural features.

Work a jig or minnow around all visible cover and fish-concentrating structure—stumps, fallen and standing timber, rocks, man-made brush piles and the like. If most crappie are caught around features at the point's shallower end, then concentrate on shallow features when you move to other areas. Likewise, if crappie seem to be favoring deeper areas on the point, continue fishing deep-water structure until you notice a shift in the pattern.

Working jigs in and around flooded sticks of beaver lodges is a good way to zero in on crappie.

Shallow Ledges and Channel Breaks

Crappie anglers always should watch their fish finder for signs of shallow ledges and channel breaks beneath the water. These aren't deep drop-offs that fall away 10 feet or more along a major river channel, but rather shallow ditches, cuts, ledges and gullies often found near bankside bluffs or close to coves and bays. These structures are especially productive when associated with nearby weed-beds, timber stands or other crappie cover.

Beaver Lodges

Crappie love beaver lodges, and they often hide in the dense woody tangles created when beavers lay sticks to build a home. Because this type of cover is so dense, you'll probably have to work it with a jig and jigging pole. Some crappie will be in shallow cover, but most big crappie will be on the outer edges of the lodge where the sticks disappear into deeper water.

Fish Shelters

Fisheries agencies often construct elaborate fish shelters by sinking reefs of trees and brush in waters where lack of cover has limited fish production. Buoys mark the locations of most shelters. Others are marked on maps and can be pinpointed using a fish finder. All such shelters are likely to harbor crappie concentrations year-round.

Cypress Trees

Crappie gather around bald cypresses wherever these water-loving trees are found. They won't be around the same trees year-round, however. When the spring spawn is underway, you'll find more crappie by fishing cypresses in shallow shoreline waters. In summer and winter, you'll do better fishing trees standing in or near deeper water. Autumn may find crappie deep or shallow, so fish cypress trees in a variety of places, deep and shallow.

In waters with hundreds of cypresses, narrow the scope of your search to particular types of trees. Cypress trees standing alone or in small clusters offshore often indicate the presence of an underwater hump (a favorite crappie haunt) and always

The knees and broad bases of cypress trees should be checked for crappie wherever they are found.

are worth trying. Trees with big open hollows also should be checked as big crappie love to hide in the dark interiors to ambush prey fish passing by. Also focus your attention on the outermost cypress trees on points, trees with lots of tall knees erupting from the water some distance from the buttressed trunk and big cypress stumps with hollow interiors.

Flooded Willows

When fishing big rivers and their backwaters, you can bet your bottom dollar you'll always find crappie holding around inundated willow trees. Fishing the outermost willows in these areas is the best way to catch lots of big crappie, but if that fails, work other portions of the willow stand. Be attentive, too, to long rows of flooded willows on natural lakes where overflows raise the water level. These are hotspots not to be missed.

Inundated Lakes and Ponds

Small ponds and lakes inundated when larger lakes fill are prime locales for crappie year-round. These offer easy access to deep-water holding areas and shallow feeding spots. They're especially productive in large shallow lakes.

Pinpoint the spot with sonar, then look within it for points, drop-offs, sunken islands or humps that attract crappie. If scattered trees or stumps exist around the perimeter, fish them carefully.

Threadfin Shad Schools

Threadfin shad schools almost always are followed by loose groups of big crappie, and sometimes schools of smaller fish. When the lake you're fishing is inhabited by threadfins (check with the local fisheries department or knowledgeable anglers), watch for clues to help you pinpoint the baitfish.

As a general rule, look for shad schools in deeper water throughout winter and around midday during warm seasons. Look in shallower water near dawn and dusk in spring, summer and fall. You may see shad leaping or swirling as predator fish chase them. On a fish finder, a school of threadfins usually appears as a band of pixels one to several feet thick. Crappie will appear as scattered individuals around or beneath the shad, seldom more than half a dozen or so together. Find them, and you can target them with appropriate lures.

Isolated Stumps

You'll rarely go wrong working a jig or minnow around any stumps isolated from other types of structure. If you can find an area with lots of widely scattered stumps,

Crappie anglers often find their quarry near isolated bits of cover and structure such as stumps in open water.

so much the better. Fish each stump thoroughly on all sides, targeting the shady side first on sunny days.

The best stumps often are those barely visible beneath the water's surface, but you'll have to move slowly and watch carefully to find them. Anglers often carry short lengths of cane to stick in the tops of such stumps as markers. It's then easier to come back and fish the stumps throughout the day.

Inflow Water-Control Structures

Many crappie waters have water-control structures bringing an inflow of fresh water to the main water body. This may be a pipe jutting from a bank with water pouring out the end, an underwater well head that creates a boil in an otherwise calm surface or a big culvert with a fresh inflow of rain after a shower. Baitfish such as shad gather in the well-oxygenated water around these structures, and crappie gather to eat the baitfish. Working spinners and spoons through areas where the water is disturbed is one good way to catch these often scattered slabs.

Thicket Structures

In waters where the edges of good crappie cover get pounded by scores of anglers, the biggest crappie often move inside dense cover stands (thickets) to avoid the ruckus. For example, if a lake has acres of button willows, slabs rarely are caught along the easily reached edges of these bushes. To find them, anglers must pull their boats into the thicket and target particular types of structure within that attract crappie. This may be log or stump, the edge of a creek channel meandering through or perhaps a cluster of standing snags. Any structure different from the norm is likely to attract crappie here.

When trophy crappie are your target, don't overlook these hotspots, regardless of the time of year. They're difficult to reach and difficult to fish, but a jig or minnow dropped inside a thicket will nearly always entice a slab.

Humps

Locating an underwater hump is like finding a map to buried treasure for the crappie fan. These structures are among the most productive crappie spots in any lake year-round.

Studying a bottom contour map of the body of water you plan to fish helps you pinpoint structures such as humps, where crappie are likely to be.

A bottom contour map helps in finding humps. Look in areas near old river channels and large feeder creeks for concentric rings of contour lines. If the depth numbers grow progressively smaller when moving toward the center of the circles, it's a hump. If the depth grows larger, you've found a depression, and it, too, may be worth investigating.

When you've pinpointed the hump with sonar, learn all you can about it—its size, the steepness of drops on each side, existing cover and so forth. Narrow your fishing area to a few choice zones—points, pockets, rock beds, timbered or brushy areas, etc.—then mark them with buoys or with a waypoint on your GPS.

The best humps are 5 to 20 feet from the surface and have substantial deep water around them, such as a creek channel running alongside. Humps with timber, brush, rocks or other cover also are productive.

We've discussed only twelve hotspots; there are dozens more. What's important to remember is this: the best bait and equipment are useless unless hungry crappie are nearby. If you take time to find the best areas, however, and present your bait in the right manner, the odds improve for catching lots of crappie, including occasional trophies.

MASTERING ELECTRONICS

Crappie guide Darryl Morris takes clients fishing year-round on several west-central Arkansas lakes. This veteran angler says a key factor in pinpointing crappie each season is fine-tuning and mastering your electronics so you can identify the exact depth and structure where fish are holding.

"Your sonar unit is like your eyes underwater," Morris says. "No matter which unit you have, learning to use it fully aids you in catching more crappie this season."

Begin by correctly setting the unit's sensitivity.

"Most units have two sensitivity settings: one for the unit overall and another for the fish ID," says Morris. "If your unit is set correctly, you should be able to get a sonar return on a small jig but not identify it as a fish.

"To do this, drop a jig into the unit's cone. Turn your sensitivity down until it disappears, and then back up until it reappears as a fine line on your screen. As you move the jig up and down, turn the fish ID sensitivity down until it stops identifying it as a fish. Your unit is now set, and you can have confidence what you see is true."

Next, you should set your unit's depth offset.

"If your transducer is 1 foot under the water's surface, your depth offset should be +1," says Morris. "But don't stop there; check it for accuracy. On a calm day, drop a bank sinker to hard bottom, mark the line at the water's surface and measure the actual depth. Adjust your depth offset accordingly. Now learn the relationship between your depth reading and the grid lines. Have confidence you can precisely read the depth at which fish are holding."

When your sensitivities and depth offset are perfect, you must learn to correctly interpret the sonar return.

"Learn to distinguish fish and cover, and learn to read a fish's sonar return when the fish is in the cover," Morris says. "Newer color units make this simpler by displaying different colors for varying densities. Also, understand that when the boat is moving or the fish is swimming through the cone, a nice arch will form. Otherwise, when movement is minimal, the sonar return is a flatter, longer line as opposed to an arch.

"Ultimately, your skill should grow from just finding fish to targeting specific groups of fish at specific depths. Such abilities will put more crappie in your livewell because you'll no longer waste time fishing 5 feet above the fish or 10 feet below them. You'll be able to identify the fish and know exactly the depth where you should present your lure. Your catch rate will soar."

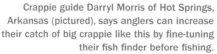

Crappie guide Darryl Morris of Hot Springs, Arkansas (pictured), says anglers can increase their catch of big crappie like this by fine-tuning their fish finder before fishing.

SECTION II

TACKLE TIPS

POLES

Fishing with long cane poles or jigging poles will often produce more fish per unit of effort than fishing with spinning or spincast tackle, especially when fishing heavy cover where casting is next to impossible.

Cane was the preferred long pole material for many years, and cane poles are still standard crappie-fishing tackle nationwide. Some excellent jigging poles manufactured with modern materials have evolved, however, and taken away much of the cane market. These are much more durable and offer better "feel." They are superb for working jigs and other small lures in hard-to-reach spots.

Most jigging poles are made of fiberglass, graphite or graphite composites. Fiberglass is more durable than graphite but lacks graphite's remarkable sensitivity. It also is heavier and bends more easily with the same amount of pull. Graphite is lighter and stiffer and is more expensive than fiberglass. Graphite/fiberglass composites offer the best of both worlds—strength, sensitivity, flexibility and moderate pricing.

Some jigging poles have a reel built into the butt, with the line run through the inside of the pole and out the tip. Dismantling and reassembling the rig when line gets short or tangled behind the reel seat can be difficult, though. The best choice for most anglers is a pole outfitted with an ultralight underspin reel or a small line holder. These can be taped to the pole if a reel seat is not provided. They are easily spooled with the proper line size, and line still can be adjusted to suit fishing conditions.

Long poles are important crappie-angling tools, useful for fishing open water, dense cover and everything in between.

Jigging poles vary from 8 to 20 feet long, but the longest poles are often too heavy and awkward for comfortable use. A light, limber 10- to 12-foot pole is usually the best model for catching crappie in brushy hideaways.

POLE TIPS

- Carry crappie poles in a variety of sizes, long and short, for use in different situations. For example, a 10-foot pole may work fine for jigging around cover in water that has become stained after a rain, but if the water is clear and crappie seem persnickety, you may do better using a 14-foot pole that allows you to fish from a greater distance.
- Crappie poles often come in telescoping models, with sections that slide one inside the other to reduce the original length. These may be better than one-piece or two-piece poles when travel space is at a premium.
- Replacement tips often are available for crappie poles that have line guides. Keep a few in your tackle box along with some glue to make on-the-water repairs.
- Crappie poles that have slide rings for seating the reel allow you to move the reel up or down the handle to a spot that provides more balance. After the rings are properly positioned, they can be secured using electrical tape.
- If you want better line control when pole fishing, your line should be about the same length as the pole to which you attach it.

When fishing from shore, a longer pole may be more advantageous for fishing nearby hotspots. Longer poles allow you to fish your bait or lure vertically from a greater distance so you get fewer snags.

PRO TIP

"Four tips can help your long-pole jigging for crappie. First, use a sensitive graphite pole because you will feel more bites and therefore catch more fish. Two, use a high-visibility line. You will get as many bites as on clear line, but you will see more bites when your line twitches or moves sideways. Three, paint a 1-inch color band near the tip of your pole. For example, if your pole is dark, use fluorescent white or yellow paint. The contrast will make seeing the tip easier when the sun is reflecting brightly off the water or at dusk when you have the tip shoved into the dark reaches of a bush. Four, keep your rod tip near the water for better bait control and to keep the wind from swaying your line."

—Tim Huffman, www.monstercrappie.com

RODS AND REELS

Choosing a rod and reel combo for crappie fishing is like buying a vehicle. Hundreds of styles and combinations are available, everything from simple, inexpensive models to top-of-the-line imports with lots of bells and whistles. Not every angler needs or wants the same thing. Before you buy, consider these facts.

Rods

Two of the most important considerations in selecting a rod are the power rating (ultralight, light, medium, etc.) and the action (fast, medium, slow).

When considering power, remember that ultralight rods are best for line weights of 1- to 4-pound-test and lures weighing 1/64 to 1/16 ounce. Light rods are best for line weights of 4- to 8-pound-test and lures weighing 1/32 to 1/8 ounce. These two types are used by most crappie anglers who fish with a rod and reel, although medium-weight rods (for lines of 4- to 12-pound-test and lures weighing 1/8 to 3/8 ounce) sometimes are used as well.

"Action" is the term used to describe the flexibility or stiffness a rod exhibits. Three actions are available:

Fast-Action: This style bends very little; in fact, only the tip section will actually bend. A rod of this type is ideal when targeting large gamefish but isn't suited for crappie fishing.

Medium-Action: A medium-action rod is the most common choice when the angler will be using various applications for a variety of species. These rods bend for about half their length, allowing an angler to fish both for small and large species with good control and hooksetting allowances.

Slow-Action: A slow-action rod bends throughout nearly its whole length, providing the most flexible action available. These rods are used almost exclusively for panfish such as crappie, allowing a better fight for the angler. They also provide "shock absorber" action so the hook is not ripped through the mouth when set, an important characteristic when fishing for "paper-mouths."

Crappie anglers often opt for a light spincast or spinning combo, which allows longer casts with light lures.

Before purchasing, you also should consider the rod's composition (fiberglass, graphite or graphite composite), just as you would the composition of a pole (see characteristics under "Poles").

When selecting a rod, keep these facts in mind as well. Spinning rods allow greater casting distance when using light lures. They have a different action than spincast rods. They also are better for landing fish on light line because there is significantly less friction caused by the guides. Spinning rod guides are on the underside of the blank. For these reasons, spinning tackle usually is the best choice if the angler using the outfit has no trouble casting with this type of combo.

Reels

Reels are available in three basic types: baitcasting, spinning and spincast.

While baitcasting reels once were considered largely unsuitable for fishing the light lines, small lures and tiny baits typically used when crappie fishing, many of today's anglers frequently use them when spider trolling with heavier lures such as crankbaits and spinners. Many pro anglers favor baitcasters for two-handed, two-pole, vertical fishing techniques and for faster gear ratios that allow crappie to be landed more quickly.

Spinning reels, sometimes called open-face reels, are an ideal choice when casting or bait fishing because they handle smaller diameter lines well. However, spincast reels (also called push-button reels) are still the traditional favorites of many crappie fans. Spincast reels offer simple push-button casting control with a soft delivery suita-

Spinning reels (left) work best with smaller diameter lines, but many crappie anglers still favor a spincast reel (right), which offers simpler casting and control.

ble for minnows and other natural baits. And because they're simpler to use and rarely backlash or tangle, they're perfect for children and novice adults learning to cast.

Crappie anglers also use a wide variety of "line-holder" reels. These are not used for casting but provide line storage and quick line length adjustment on poles used primarily for jig or minnow fishing. Most are much less expensive than other reel types. No-frills plastic models are available, but more durable, versatile versions have metal or graphite components and features such as Teflon drags, anti-reverse levers, audible clickers, quick-change line spools, right- or left-hand retrieve, larger spool capacity and faster gear ratios.

ROD TIPS

- Sensitive rods help you detect more light-biting crappie. One way to determine if you have a rod that is truly sensitive is to rub the rod tip lightly across some corduroy cloth. If your rod is sensitive, you'll feel the material's texture.
- Check the guides on each rod before every fishing trip. If any are bent, straighten them, or line will not flow through correctly. Also, take a cotton swab and turn it inside each guide. If any cotton sticks to the inner portion of the guide, replace the guide before you use the rod again. If you do not, the line will fray or become nicked and could break when you set the hook on a crappie.
- When using a two-piece rod, rub a very light coating of paraffin onto the ferrule. This not only makes for a firm, secure connection, but also makes it easier to separate the sections.
- At home, it's best to store rods in a horizontal or vertical rack. Don't lean them against a wall or stack in a corner. If you do, each rod could become permanently bowed.
- When motoring from one spot to another, always lay your rods flat. If you lean a rod against a sharp edge, the bouncing of the boat may score the blank, causing it to break when a fish is on.

You can coat cork rod handles with Armor All Original Protectant to keep them soft and clean.

REEL TIPS

- If you can't cast as far as you need to, switch to a spinning reel with a long-cast-style spool that is longer and shallower. On most reels, line flows freely when you first cast, but as the line level drops on the spool, the line must climb a steeper grade over the spool lip. This increased friction reduces the distance you can cast. With a long-cast spool, the shallower design keeps the lip smaller, thus casting distances are improved.

- When setting your reel's drag, always do so by pulling line off the end of the rod, not directly off the reel's spool. That will give you the proper tension.

- When dismantling a reel for cleaning, place each part in a separate compartment of an empty egg carton as you go along. When reassembling the reel, pick up the parts in reverse order.

- Anglers using spinning reels often experience line-twist problems. When this happens, remove your lure, release 100 feet of line and drag the line behind your boat while idling. When you have moved a short distance, retie. Your problem is solved.

- Proper reel maintenance includes regular lubrication of all moving parts such as bearings, spool spindles and gears. Lubricate lightly, however, and do not use heavy oil, oil with a lot of wax or other additives, or grease. These can gum up or leave a residue that inhibits movement of the bearings and other close-tolerance parts. Fine, light lubricants such as Rem Oil and X1R reel lube are excellent choices.

HOW TO STUFF A CRAPPIE TACKLE BOX

My uncle, Guy McClintock, spent much of his life fishing for crappie. His fishing vessel was a 10-foot johnboat handcrafted from cypress. His poles were hand-cut canes.

Not surprisingly, the tackle box he used was equally domestic—a coffee can into which he stuffed a few hooks, several yards of dacron fishing line, some small corks and an aspirin bottle filled with split shot.

A crappie fan who fishes like my uncle did—with minnows and cane poles—may need nothing more than a simple little tackle box to store terminal tackle and line. A coffee can will suffice, although you may want something even simpler, like a shoe box or Ziploc bag.

If you're like me, though, minnows and cane poles aren't enough to satisfy. I frequently fish with shiners, but I also like working jigs, spoons, crankbaits, spinners and other crappie lures. I still love fishing with cane poles, but there are times when I'd rather be casting with a spinning combo or working heavy brush with a jigging pole. If crappie are hard to entice, I may switch lures and poles several times, trying to find the perfect combination. Consequently, I prefer a large tackle box in which to carry all my fishing paraphernalia.

Here's some advice for selecting and stuffing a tackle box ideal for crappie fishing.

The Tackle Box

There are innumerable styles of tackle boxes on today's market. The one you select will depend largely on how much tackle you carry on each outing, the type of tackle you use and, if you're budget-conscious, the price.

A big tackle bag that holds several plastic boxes with dividers is ideal for carrying the many lures, hooks, bobbers and other small items of tackle used by most crappie anglers.

If you're primarily a minnow fisherman, a small box to accommodate a selection of hooks, bobbers, sinkers and line may suit your needs perfectly. But if you fish both jigs and minnows, you'll probably want something more elaborate.

I tried a variety of tackle boxes—cloth bags, over-and-unders, tilt-trays and more—before finding my favorite. Most didn't have enough tray compartments to organize my jigs. And those that had an ample number of compartments didn't have space for larger tackle such as line spools and extra reels.

In the end, I settled on a large cloth tackle bag that holds several worm-proof plastic boxes, each with dividers that can be custom-fit to create up to 24 compartments. I've configured the dividers so I have more than 100 compartments in which to organize different colors and sizes of jigs and jigheads, plus all the other lures and tackle I carry. The tackle bag also has several large pockets where I can store bulkier gear like stringers, line and reels.

Check out the variety of tackle boxes and bags available through your sporting-goods dealer, study them to determine what type best suits your needs, then invest in a top-quality model and fill it with tackle to create your own ultimate crappie box. Here are some things you'll need to get started.

Terminal Tackle

In my tackle bag, I keep a small compartmented box for organizing hooks, sinkers and bobbers.

I prefer No. 6 Aberdeen cricket hooks and No. 1, 1/0 and 2/0 gold Aberdeen minnow hooks. I keep several dozen of each size, mostly thin wire models that do the least damage to fragile minnows and will bend enough to free from snags when fishing brush.

Split shot are the primary type of sinkers I use. I prefer those with small "ears" for easier removal and generally have 100 or more in sizes 8 to 3 in my bag.

Bobbers, or floats, also are important items of crappie equipment. In addition to suspending the bait at the right depth and providing a visual cue that a fish has taken the bait, they also add weight so you can better cast those tiny 1/64- to 1/32-ounce lures. I

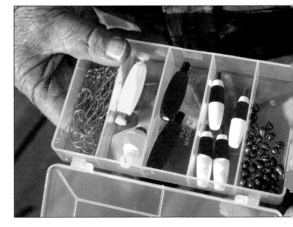

Crappie anglers who fish primarily with minnows may need only a small tackle box containing a few bobbers, sinkers and hooks.

It's a good idea to keep a variety of jigs in different colors, sizes and styles.

usually keep 15 to 20 in my tackle bag, including fixed bobbers and slip bobbers made with foam, balsa and cork.

I keep an extra spool of 4- to 8-pound test line for situations dictating light line and a spool of 17-pound line I use when fishing heavy brush. I use premium mono-filament and consider fluorescent green or yellow line best. These colors are more visible, which permits detection of the lightest strikes.

Jigs and Other Lures

Jigs are my favorite crappie lures. To be prepared for any situation, my tackle bag contains several styles, colors and weights. Ninety percent are 1/32-ounce, because that's the size I find most productive in most situations. However, there are times and places where smaller or larger jigs prove more productive, so I carry a variety of larger and smaller models as well.

I also keep an assortment of small safety-pin spinners in my tackle bag. These can be snapped on a jig to add extra crappie-attracting flashiness and vibration in stained or muddy water. In addition, I carry a small selection of other crappie-catching lures to use when jig fishing isn't productive. Among my favorites are 1/8- to 1/4-ounce spoons, mini-crankbaits, small in-line and horsehead spinners and bladebaits.

Miscellaneous Equipment

The remaining equipment in my crappie bag consists of these items: an extra line-holder reel that will fit any of my jigging poles, an extra ultralight spinning reel, two stringers, a Berkley multi-tool, reel oil, sunscreen, nail clippers (for trimming line), a digital fish scale, a fish-scaler tool, a fillet knife and a ceramic knife sharpener. That's it. I have everything I need for most outings, and it's all together in a small package ready for transport.

Of course, there's no limit to the number of interesting items you can find to enhance your crappie fishing. And if you're like me, you'll be continually adding to your collection of "must-have" paraphernalia.

A few examples of the many useful "miscellaneous" items you may want to include in your crappie-fishing gear: Schrade Folding Fillet Knife, Berkley Mini Fishing Tool, Smith's JIFF-FISH with built-in scale, tape measure and hook hone, Berkley Deluxe Rod Tip Repair Kit.

OPTIONAL ITEMS

Here are some additional items you may want to add to your crappie tackle:

- Bottom contour maps of your favorite fishing lakes
- Lighted floats for night fishing
- Fillet knife
- Pocket-size rain poncho
- Hook hone
- Fishing towel
- Emergency rod tip repair kit
- Battery-operated reel stripper
- Small marker buoys
- Compact binoculars
- Small, waterproof disposable camera
- Portable GPS unit
- Outboard motor repair kit with tools
- First-aid kit
- Small flashlight and/or signal flares
- Waterproof matches or butane lighter

TACKLE BOX TIPS

- Save those little packets of silica gel that come packaged with many electronic products. A few placed in your tackle box will absorb moisture and help prevent mildew.
- Movable dividers in plastic tackle boxes sometimes slide up, allowing small tackle items to get combined. Put some silicone sealer on the bottom of each divider to hold it in place. You still can easily remove the divider to redesign or clean the box.
- It's a good practice to empty and clean your tackle boxes at the end of each season. Wash the boxes with mild detergent, get rid of unusable lures, terminal tackle, etc., and allow the boxes to dry thoroughly before replacing the good stuff.

The small plastic tubes and clear plastic boxes many candies come in are great for storing and separating weights, hooks, rattles, beads and other terminal tackle.

LINE TIPS

- Fishing line can be ruined by direct sunlight or heat inside a vehicle. Keep reels and spools of line in cool, dark places when you're not on the water.
- Sometimes it's necessary to put new line on a reel while you're on the water. When this is done, many anglers keep the new line tight by running it through their hand or a wrapped towel. It's ok to do this, but be careful not to hold the line too tight. Heat generated by friction on the moving line can weaken the line. To be sure the line stays cool, you should wet your hand or the towel before you begin.
- Keep a coffee can with a big X cut in the plastic lid where you can stuff scrap fishing line after retying or respooling.

The credit card–shaped letter openers available at many office supply stores are great line cutters, even for braided line, and fit inside a shirt pocket.

BOBBER TIPS

- When crappie seem unusually persnickety, switch from the brightly colored bobber you typically use to a clear casting bubble like those used by trout anglers. The transparent float is harder for the angler to see, but also less visible to fish, thus increasing hookups.
- Can't quite reach that bed of spooky spawning crappie from a distance? Switch from a regular bobber to a weighted bobber for the extra heft you need to go the distance.
- An illuminated bobber may be just what you need to detect bites when night fishing. Many types now are available, such as Gamakatsu's Firetip Float with a highly visible LED light and Cabela's Lighted Adjust-a-Bubble with glow sticks that insert in the top. For a cheaper option, use a small rubber band or tape to affix one of Thill's Bobber Brite Glow Sticks to the top of any bobber.

Crappie often swim upward after inhaling a bait. Your bobber never moves, which leads to missed fish. Catch these light biters by using a "waggler" (antenna-type bobber) like Thill's Stealth Float on 2- to 4-pound-test line. Attach the float to your line, tie on a jig or minnow hook and then start adding small split shot between the hook and float. Use enough weight so only 1/4-inch of the bobber protrudes above the water when you drop it in. If a crappie swims upward after grabbing the bait, it removes some weight off the line, and the super-sensitive bobber rises enough to clearly indicate a taker.

HOOK TIPS

- Most crappie anglers prefer hooks made with wire that is relatively thin. If the wire has too great a diameter, your bait may die or swim unnaturally, and the hook won't bend enough to pull free when snagged.
- Sharp hooks catch more crappie. Check hook sharpness by dragging the hook across one of your fingernails. A hook that sticks or scratches the nail is sharp; one that doesn't isn't and should be honed.
- Safety pins or paper clips can be used to hold and separate hooks of various sizes.

If your eyesight is no longer so hot, use an old-fashioned needle-threader to help thread line through hooks. Push the loop of the needle-threader through the hook eye, then drop your line through the loop and pull it back through—fast, simple and free of aggravation.

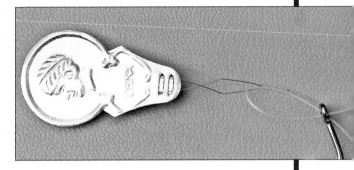

PRO TIP

"Instead of the big gold minnow hooks most crappie anglers use, I prefer No. 6 light-wire Aberdeen cricket hooks because they allow me to fish brush with fewer hang-ups. Snagged cricket hooks also will straighten on the 8-pound line I use without disturbing my brush piles, and they allow me to use smaller minnows, which often are more effective than large minnows."

—Jerry Blake, www.actionfishingtrips.com

SECTION III

LURE SELECTION

PICK THE PERFECT JIG

The diversity of crappie jigs is mind-boggling. Thousands of styles and colors are available. Jigs come with bodies of rubber, plastic, marabou, hair, rubber bands, floss, tinsel, chenille and other materials. They may be shaped like minnows, shad, grubs, worms or innumerable other creatures. There are jigs with curly tails, ripple tails, broad tails and triple tails; jigs with lead heads, floating heads, diving heads and standing heads; jigs with spinners and without spinners; weedless jigs and those that aren't; and all this in every color in the rainbow and every combination imaginable.

This presents a dilemma for crappie anglers. How do you select the jig that will catch the most crappie? Are there certain conditions when one lure is preferable over another? When are big jigs more appropriate? Small ones? Is a jig with a spinner better or one without? Should a weedless jig be used or not?

There are no pat answers to these questions. I've seen days when crappie would hit everything from a 1/100-ounce squirrel hair jig to a 1-ounce bass model. I've also seen days when crappie were so finicky they'd refuse all but a single offering. A black /red/yellow soft-plastic tube jig might work, but a black/red/yellow marabou jig would not.

So, what's an angler to do? Start by applying the following general guidelines when choosing jigs. You'll find these rules of thumb productive more often than not. On those occasions when they fail, don't fret. Yes, crappie can be persnickety. But if they're actively feeding and you try enough variations, sooner or later you'll find the perfect combination.

Matching the Hatch, So to Speak

One key to catching crappie consistently is using lures matching the size of the natural forage the fish are accustomed to eating. If you present a 1-inch jig to a school of crappie

Jigs are the most popular and effective of all crappie lures, so it's important to know how to select the right jig from the many varieties available.

It's always smart to match jigs to the size of the predominant forage in the body of water you're fishing. For example, if 2-inch minnows comprise a large part of the crappie diet, use jigs the same size.

feeding on 2-inch baitfish, there's a good chance you won't hook up. In fact, many expert anglers contend that imitating the size and shape of natural forage is more important to success than picking the right lure color.

How do you decide which size and shape is best? Because the predominant forage fish vary considerably from one body of water to another, from season to season and even from day to day, the best way is to look at the stomach contents of crappie you catch. When you land a slab, see what's inside. If the fish is stuffed with tiny shiners, lures of that same general size and shape most likely will produce. The same holds true with other forage, such as shad or fathead minnows.

There will be times, of course, when you can't use this method because the crappie simply won't cooperate. In that case, try applying these general seasonal guidelines.

Spring

Crappie begin spawning activity when the water temperature is around 56 degrees. This occurs before most baitfish spawn. Consequently, most forage fish available for spawning crappie to eat are quite large. Some crappie will eat largemouth bass fry, which have just become available, but for the most part, food animals are larger than they will be during other seasons. For this reason, when fishing for bedding crappie, it is wise to mimic the predominant natural forage and use larger jigs. Versions up to 1/4 ounce and 3 inches long produce well this season if slab crappie are your targets.

Big jigs produce in spring for another reason as well. Nesting crappie won't tolerate minnows or other small fish near their beds. So you'll often hit pay dirt when you present a soft-plastic jig that has a big minnow- or shad-imitation body. The crappie will make a defensive strike to rid the nest site of the intruder, and you can savor the battle.

In early spring, before forage fish such as shad and minnows have spawned, opting to use larger jigs may work to the crappie angler's advantage.

Baitfish forming the bulk of the crappie's diet—shad and several species of minnows, for example—don't spawn until after crappie have spawned, when the water warms to 70 degrees. Spawning may continue at intervals throughout warm months, usually ceasing if the water temperature rises above 80 degrees or falls below 70 degrees. The bulk of spawning activity, however, occurs from mid-April through early June in mid-latitudes, and a bit earlier or later to the south and north.

When baitfish hatch, crappie suddenly have many sizes of forage animals on which to feed, from tiny fry to jumbo adults. After just a few days, however, the number of small baitfish far exceeds the number of adults. Crappie gorge on this bounty of fresh fry, stuffing themselves after a winter on lean rations.

Because crappie are eating mostly small forage fish, you'll probably catch more crappie by changing over to smaller jigs. When the water temperature is still near 70 degrees, most baitfish fry will still be tiny, and tiny jigs—1/100 to 1/64 ounce, 1 inch or less—probably will be most enticing. By the time the water temperature rises above 75 degrees, many juvenile baitfish will exceed 1-inch long, and you may want to upsize your jigs to match this growth. A 1/32- or 1/16-ounce jig, 1 to 1-1/2 inches long, may now work as well as something smaller.

Summer

As spring turns to summer, baitfish near adult size. A threadfin shad, for example, may be 2 inches long at the first growing season's end. A gizzard shad may reach 5 inches. This means crappie have many larger baitfish on which to feed. In fact, from now through early autumn, large baitfish will be at peak abundance.

This is not to say, however, big jigs are best this season. They certainly may work, but during summer, baitfish continue spawning periodically, and fry remain an abundant food source. Thus, crappie are regularly eating large baitfish and small. If the waters you fish don't get too hot too early, and if there's a good mix of large and small crappie, this is the one time of year when you can use any size jig and still expect consistent action.

It's important to remember, however, that much depends on the size of crappie available. For example, many waters are crowded with small crappie. In these, you may need to stick with smaller jigs—nothing over 1/32 or 1/16 ounce or 1 inch long— regardless of the season because an 8-ounce crappie is less likely to inhale a 1/8-ounce jig than a 2-pound crappie. Where crappie reach larger sizes, however, with a good mix of slabs and "barely keepers," stick with the seasonal guidelines presented here.

Autumn and Winter

In early autumn, expect summer patterns to continue. Crappie still find baitfish in many sizes and may strike a jig regardless of its size. As the water temperature falls,

In winter, when crappie bite slow-moving or stationary lures best, you can slow your jig presentation by downsizing the leadhead you use with a particular body style.

however, baitfish spawning activities cease, and the number of small baitfish drops as these fish grow or succumb to predation and cold weather. By the time winter is in full swing, the baitfish still alive tend to be larger on average than baitfish at other times.

This being the case, one would suspect that jigs with a larger silhouette would entice more winter crappie. I've found this to be true in the waters I fish, but only when the jigs are configured to allow a very slow presentation. The crappie's metabolism plunges when water temperature falls, and the fish often refuse to chase lures, even for short distances. Thus, jigs used to entice them must be presented very slowly. The lure should enter the fish's strike zone and remain there for best results.

This explains why many anglers downsize jigs in winter, even though most forage fish are large. The most elementary way to slow a lure's descent is to reduce the lure's size. Micro-jigs of 1/64 ounce and smaller drop through the water column at the agonizingly slow rate winter crappie prefer. Heavier jigs fall faster, often descending too quickly for lethargic crappie to strike. It would seem to make sense then that smaller lures would work better.

That might be true if downsizing your jig was the only way to slow it. But it's not. Another simple method is to use heavier line. Heavier line causes more resistance in the water, causing jigs to fall more slowly. In clear water, where line-shy fish are a concern, an easy solution is adding a foot or two of lighter leader between the main line and the jig. Another effective approach for reducing the fall rate is using a larger jig body (one bigger than what normally would be matched with a given jighead size) to create increased water resistance.

A bobber presents yet another means for fishing a jig slowly. A float rig allows the jig to be suspended, which means it can be worked at almost any pace, including a dead stop. If crappie are holding deeper than 6 feet, as they tend to do in winter, casting with a traditional float might be impractical. But a slip bobber serves the same basic function and can be rigged with a bobber stop so it suspends your jig at the correct depth.

Knowing these things, we now can do a better job matching our jig to the size of most baitfish being eaten by cold-water crappie. If a stomach analysis finds crappie stuffed with 2-inch shad, we can present a 2-inch, wide-bodied jig beneath a float, and work it very slowly at the depth crappie are suspended. When crappie forage consists primarily of large minnows, we can slow the presentation of properly matched jigs by using 15- or even 20-pound test line, with an added leader if necessary, or by using a 1/32-ounce jighead on a jig body more often used with a 1/16-ounce jighead. And so on.

Other Considerations

It would be nice if the guidelines given above would work every time we go crappie fishing. Unfortunately, they won't. Successful crappie anglers consider many other facts as well.

For example, water clarity in the lake or reservoir we're fishing will considerably influence the right jig choice. In muddy water, crappie rely more on sound, vibrations and odor to find food. Thus, adding a spinner or rattling jighead to each jig may improve success. Clear-water crappie, on the other hand, can better detect phony offerings, so it may be best to stick with smaller jigs they can't see as well. Jigs weighing 1/32 ounce usually outproduce 1/16-ounce jigs in this situation. Likewise, a 1/64-ounce jig may be better than a 1/32-ounce jig.

Are crappie hidden away in dense cover? If so, you may need to switch over to a weedless jig like Charlie Brewer's Crappie Slider. Are they feeding heavily on some type of insect or crustacean that's suddenly become abundant? Perhaps you should think about using a jig that more closely mimics one of these forage animals.

Sometimes crappie gather in dam tailwaters or other areas with heavy current. If so, you may need a heavier jig for proper presentation. A heavier jig also may help you reach deep summer and winter crappie more quickly.

When the fish get especially persnickety, you may need added enticements such as a curly tail or a jig where the soft-plastic body covers the entire leadhead. Scented jig bodies may be a bonus, or luminescent ones when fishing at night.

The variables you'll encounter are nearly endless. But that's why the variety of jigs is nearly endless as well. If you carry a tackle box with a wide variety of styles and colors, and experiment with several variations, sooner or later you'll find the perfect combination.

Smart crappie anglers carry a wide assortment of jig colors, sizes and styles. Varying what is used can help the fisherman determine what works best for the conditions encountered.

JIG TIPS

- The best jig fishermen have a high level of concentration, a fine-tuned sense of feel and quick reflexes. If you fail to pay constant attention, if you aren't accustomed to recognizing subtle strikes or if you don't set the hook immediately upon getting a taker, you're not likely to catch many crappie.

- If you hook a crappie in the thin membrane around its mouth, the hook can tear out easily. To help eliminate this problem, bend the jig hook about 10 degrees outward from its original position. The hook is now more likely to stick in the roof of the crappie's mouth than in the membrane.

- Tired of losing jigs to snags? Carry along a 1-ounce bell sinker with a snap attached to the brass eye. When a jig gets hung, clip the sinker on your line and drop it. When the sinker hits the lure, it usually dislodges it. If not, jiggle your pole so the sinker bounces against the jig.

- Adding a scent product to your jigs may help you nab finicky slabs. Some products are sprayed on the outside of the lure. The best, however, are liquids or pastes you can "load" inside a tube. Do this by squeezing the tube lure, which is held with the open end up. As you inject the product into the tube, gradually release your hold on the tube. This pulls the scent inside, allowing it to be released more slowly than sprayed-on scent. Pellet-type scents can be shaped to the right size and pushed into the tube body for similar effect.

- When fishing hair jigs, Arkansas crappie guide Jerry Blake keeps a squeeze bottle full of cod-liver oil on hand and places a drop or two on his lure periodically. "Cod-liver oil works just like more

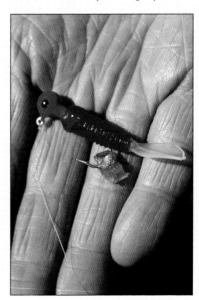

A tiny piece of minnow added to a jig hook maintains the jig's action while adding scent. Use a sharp knife to cut a fillet from the baitfish's side, then divide it lengthwise into several pieces. The added smell/taste increases your catch when finicky crappie avoid larger offerings.

expensive scents," he says, "encouraging crappie to hold the lure longer so I have a better chance of hooking them."

- If you pinpoint feeding crappie near schools of surface-running shad, try casting a 1/32-ounce jig tied above a 1/8-ounce jig with a small safety-pin spinner. The heavier jig stays well beneath the upper lure at a level where larger crappie are often holding. Double hookups are common.

- Many jigs now are available with glow-in-the-dark bodies and/or heads. Do they work? Sometimes yes, sometimes no, in my experience. But at times, when conventional jigs aren't producing, I've rigged with a luminescent version and started catching crappie after crappie. Rigging a small cyalume stick a foot or so ahead of the jig often improves effectiveness.

- An inexpensive tool for cleaning paint from jig eyes is a seam-ripper, available in sewing departments. Add a lanyard through a screw eye in the handle.

PRO TIP

"Do colors in jigs/lures/baits really make a difference? That's a constant question on the minds of crappie anglers nationwide. After more than forty years of crappie fishing, I've found crappie seem to prefer brighter or fluorescent-type skirts and leadheads on baits when there's dingy or muddy water. When fishing clear water, use skirts with subdued colors and unpainted leadheads. Dull colors such as clear with sparkle or motor oil are some good choices. However, be versatile and keep a buffet of colors in your jig box and let the fish decide which one they like best."

—Steve McCadams, www.stevemccadams.com

SPINNERS FOR CRAPPIE

S pinners are almost irresistible to crappie because they exhibit vibration, flash and motion, all of which attract a fish's attention.

The vibration factor has great significance, especially in muddy water and after dark. Water is a positive conductor of sound waves, and crappie are very sensitive to vibrations and underwater noises. When water is murky or dark, sight feeding is hindered, and crappie are more likely to strike a flashy lure that sends out lots of vibrations. Spinners do just that.

Spinners also allow fishing a greater area than can be done with jigs or minnows. This is especially significant when crappie are difficult to locate. The fisherman can tie on a spinner, cast to a likely looking spot, make a quick retrieve, and if a fish isn't caught, he can make another quick cast and retrieve in another spot. Jigs and minnows are more suited to a slow or stationary presentation and thus are less useful when trying to pinpoint crappie concentrations.

Also, because spinners are usually a little heavier than most other crappie lures, they can be cast longer distances with ultralight tackle. This allows you to stay farther away from the areas you're fishing, an especially important quality when fishing clear waters where crappie are apt to be easily spooked.

Safety-Pin Spinners

Three basic types of spinners are used for crappie fishing. One favorite is the safety-pin spinner. The "spinner" part of this lure consists of a V-shaped wire frame. At the point of the V is a small line-tie loop. A small spinner blade is attached to the end of one arm with a swivel. At the end of the other arm is a small open-and-close (like a safety pin) clip to which you attach a jig or grub. One well-known version of this lure is the Johnson Beetle-Spin.

Spinners are among the angler's best tools for catching slab crappie like this.

Safety-pin spinners like Johnson's Beetle-Spin are among the easiest to use of all crappie lures. Simply cast, retrieve and get ready for action.

Safety-pin spinners can cover a lot of territory when cast with ultralight gear, and they catch not only crappie but an enormous variety of other sportfish as well. If you're not sure what type structure is beneath the water you're fishing, or if you're trying to figure out where crappie are located, take a little spinner like this and fan cast in a big circle to find fish. As you retrieve the lure, work it over, through and beside woody cover and other crappie hideouts.

Another nice thing about safety-pin spinners is the fact it doesn't take much expertise to use them. Fishing tiny jigs on a long pole requires a great deal of finesse and patience. Without these virtues, your lure will catch more snags than fish. Safety-pin spinners, on the other hand, are relatively weedless. A youngster or inexperienced angler with little casting experience can fish successfully with them.

The secret of fishing a safety-pin spinner is retrieving the lure as slowly as possible and running it close to the fish. When fishing shallow brush, blowdowns, weeds and other visible cover, cast beyond the cover and bring the lure through it or alongside it. It pays to live dangerously and bump the cover with the lure, as this seems to excite crappie into biting.

If the jig or grub clipped to your spinner isn't producing, remove it and clip on a lure of different size or color. Some anglers even clip on flies like those used to catch trout, which, under the right circumstances (during a spring mayfly hatch, for example), make extremely effective crappie-catchers.

Horsehead Spinners

The Blakemore Road Runner, the only lure in this category, sometimes is called a horsehead spinner because the lure's leadhead has a horse-head shape. It's unique among spinner-type

The tiny blade attached to the head of the Road Runner spinner produces crappie-attracting flash and vibration.

lures because the spinner is attached beneath the head where it's more easily seen by fish striking from the side or below. The blade rarely tangles with your fishing line like those on safety-pin spinners tend to do, nor does it interfere with hookups. Several body styles and, two blade styles (Colorado and willow) are available, sizes from 1/32 to 1 ounce and in every color of the rainbow.

Road Runners have been popular crappie lures since they first became available in 1958. Ways to fish them are limited only by your imagination.

Bert Hall, the Missouri Ozarks stream fisherman who invented the little spinner, also crafted the wise slogan: "You can't fish a Road Runner wrong as long as you fish it slow." In many cases, slow *is* best, but crappie anglers shouldn't be buttonholed into fishing the Road Runner just one way. Depending on water conditions and the mood of the fish, this fabulous, famous crappie-catching lure can be fished slow or fast, deep or shallow, vertically or horizontally. The simplest method, perhaps, is just casting the lure and reeling it in at a snail's pace—just fast enough so the blade turns. You also can spider troll with Road Runners or drop one beneath your boat and fish different depths with little hops and twitches that will get a barn-door crappie's attention. The variations are endless, and half the fun of using Road Runners is experimenting with different tactics until you find a method slabs can't resist.

In-line (Weighted) Spinners

In-line, or weighted, spinners also are effective artificials for crappie. These are spinnerbaits constructed so the spinner blade revolves around a wire lure shaft rather that at the end of the shaft. Below the blade is a fairly heavy metal body that can be almost any size, shape or color. Noteworthy examples include the Mepps Aglia, the Panther Martin Spinner, Worden's Rooster Tail and the Luhr-Jensen Shyster.

Because they're usually fitted with a small treble hook, in-line spinners are easily snagged when fishing brushy cover. To avoid this problem, concentrate on open-water structures—bridge pilings, riprap, rock outcroppings, boat docks, underwater points, submerged humps, etc. In-lines also can be effectively fished along cover edges. Cast and retrieve along the borders of thickets, fish attractors, weed-beds and other likely hideouts, avoiding tangles within the structure.

Some anglers like trolling with in-line spinners, but if the troll is too fast,

In-line spinners come in hundreds of styles, colors and sizes, all of which catch crappie.

the lures are inclined to spin and thus twist the line. Better tactics are to drift-fish with a light breeze that moves your boat slowly across the lake or use an electric motor to maintain an ideal speed. Movement should be just fast enough to turn the lure's blade. Too fast and the lure "rides up" and twists your line. Too slow and the blade doesn't spin, rendering the lure ineffective. Done properly, this is an excellent technique for catching crappie suspended over inundated creek and river channels.

Spinners, like jigs and minnows, are part of the crappie buffet. And if you serve them up right, they can be every bit as effective as jigs and minnows.

THE THREE BASIC TYPES OF SPINNERS

1. SAFETY-PIN   2. HORSEHEAD   3. IN-LINE
Johnson Beetle-   Blakemore Road   Mepps Aglia
Spin   Runner

SPINNER TIPS

- Some crappie anglers like to "drop" spinners beside rock bluffs and creek channels. In this situation, a 1/16-ounce lure with a fairly large blade works best. The spinner is simply bounced down the drop-off on a tight line; rod-tip movement controls the lure's fall. While the lure falls, the blade spins, and nearby crappie are likely to take the bait on the drop. Watch your line closely for slackening or sideways movement that indicates a hit.
- When crappie are finicky, remove the grub or tube body from a safety-pin spinner and replace it with a small live minnow. This small change may increase the number of fish you hook.
- Some of the best in-line spinners for crappie are those like the Mepps Comet Minnow, which has a plastic minnow body in which the hooks are set.

- When a slower retrieve is desired, try using a sonic-type in-line spinner such as the Worden's Rooster Tail or Panther Martin. These have a blade that is concave on one end and convex on the other, so the blade turns very easily and will spin at a very slow retrieve speed.
- Check the clevis on your spinner (the U-shaped metal piece that holds the blade to the shaft) periodically to be sure it's not bent or fouled with vegetation. Straighten a bent clevis with needle-nose pliers.
- Summer mayfly hatches are common on many crappie lakes, and when they occur, crappie often move shallow to gorge on mayfly larvae and emerging adults. If you see numerous mayflies, try this combination lure. Remove the "beetle" from a 1/32- or 1/16-ounce Johnson Beetle-Spin, or use a separate safety-pin-type spinner, and attach a trout-fishing fly that resembles a mayfly or mayfly larvae. Good ones to try include emergers, the Pink Cahill, Adam's and Gold Bead Hare's Ear. Cast this spin/fly rig near bushes and low-hanging branches where the mayflies are present and bring it in with a slow, steady retrieve. You'll probably land as many bluegills as crappie, but where crappie are common, they should comprise a good portion of your catch.

Although small spinners typically are used by crappie anglers, don't overlook bass spinnerbaits for catching crappie, too. You won't catch many small fish, but these lures sometimes prove irresistible to slabs weighing 2 to 3 pounds.

PRO TIP

"When the water is stained, I like to take a Blakemore Road Runner and change the blade to a No. 3 gold willow-leaf blade. Big slabs can more easily find the customized lure in muddy to stained water."

—Kevin Rogers, Crappie USA Classic qualifier for six consecutive years

CRANKBAIT CRAPPIE

Today's savvy crappie anglers are innovative, often trying new tackle and tactics. Many have discovered that, given the right set of circumstances, crankbaits are extremely effective crappie-catchers, despite the fact few anglers use crankbaits when targeting these panfish.

Almost any small crankbait, and many large ones, can be used to entice crappie. I've used a 3-1/2-inch Smithwick Rattling Rogue with great success in some waters, and Rebel's 1/4-ounce Humpback works great on shallow-water slabs. The best crankbaits, regardless of the size you use, are those that mimic natural movements and colors of shad or other baitfish. And so that you'll be prepared no matter where crappie happen to be, it's a good idea to bring a variety of crankbaits that can be worked at different depths. Carry shallow-running, suspending and deep-diving models.

Crankbaits are very productive during the spring spawning season. Crappie are protective of their spawning beds and often hit these lures for that reason alone. Small floating/diving plugs such as Rebel's Super Teeny-R work especially well this season. These lures float up away from snags when the retrieve is stopped, a necessity when fishing thick spawning cover.

If you want to move even further toward eliminating hang-ups, fish near bridge pilings, riprap, rock outcroppings, boat docks, weed edges and underwater points and humps where snags are less of a problem. In oxbow lakes, crappie often hold near the bases of big cypress trees where crankbaits also are very effective, and hang-ups are less of a problem.

Deep-diving crankbaits are a real boon during summer, autumn and winter, when crappie are in deep-water areas. During these seasons, use sonar to locate crappie-attracting structure. Then position your boat parallel to the structure, and work your lure(s) slowly through the area.

Another time crankbaits are very effective is when summer crappie are schooling on the surface. During the dog days of July and August, schools of

In recent years, more and more anglers have begun using crankbaits to catch big crappie. Crankbaits resembling shad and other baitfish are superb enticements for these predatory panfish.

PHOTO BY Lawrence Taylor, PRADCO Fishing

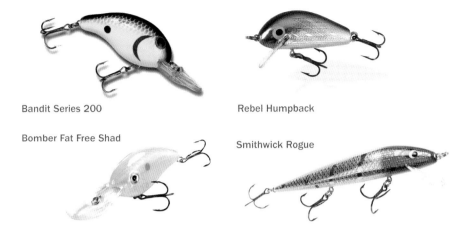

Bandit Series 200

Rebel Humpback

Bomber Fat Free Shad

Smithwick Rogue

crappie that normally hold in 15 to 25 feet of water occasionally feed at the surface of lakes or rivers at dawn and dusk. Catching them is essentially like "jump" fishing for stripers or white bass running shad, but the surfacing crappie are not as noticeable.

To find top-running crappie, look for rough patches on otherwise smooth waters in large wooded coves. The crappie usually are chasing schools of small shad, and you often can see baitfish leaping from the water where fish are feeding. Many anglers think bass are responsible for the disturbances and spend gainless hours casting large plugs at them. But by quietly positioning your boat near the feeding school and tossing a shad-imitation crankbait into the melee, you sometimes can fill an ice chest with a mess of fat slabs.

Don't expect crappie to attack crankbaits with the ferocity of bass. Often, a crappie only nips at the lure rather than hitting it hard. When you feel a crappie tapping the lure, stop reeling, drop the rod tip and take up slack. Then raise the rod on a tight line, and you usually will have the fish hooked. When the lure stops, the crappie probably thinks it has injured the prey and quickly pounces on it before one of its schoolmates grabs the easy meal.

Jigs and minnows will be the mainstays for crappie anglers as long as there are crappie to catch. Papermouth fans love to see the bobber go under and feel the bow in their jigging pole. But when crappie are just a bit finicky, when old-fashioned techniques won't produce, try the crankbait option. You may be glad you did.

Long-billed crankbaits will pluck hungry crappie from the depths where they often feed outside the spring spawning season.

CRANKBAIT TIPS

- Buoyancy determines whether a crankbait floats (positive buoyancy), sinks (negative buoyancy) or suspends (neutral buoyancy). Professional anglers are very attuned to this characteristic. When fishing heavy cover, they want baits that back up and float and have a degree of buoyancy. When fishing during cool-water periods, they want baits that can be stopped without popping back to the surface, baits that stay suspended where they are. Negative buoyancy baits like vibrating, lipless crankbaits allow you to fish all depths. You can fish them on bottom, near the top or in between. Be attuned to buoyancy to know which crankbaits to select for certain fishing conditions.

- Crappie often hold around submerged beds of green aquatic vegetation such as coontail. Test these waters for slabs by drifting or fan-casting crankbaits over the weed-beds. If the vegetation rises near the surface, use floating-minnow imitations and work them with jerky retrieves so they tickle the tops of the cover. When weed tops are separated from the surface by a few feet of water, try a suspending minnow crankbait. Where weed tops are deep, and in places where weeds are sparse, try a deeper-diving, shad-imitation crankbait worked between the stems.

- To catch crappie suspended in open water near tributary mouths, watch for boomerangs on your sonar, then try trolling crankbaits instead of jigs. Use 1/4- to 1/8-ounce divers. Silver works great on sunny days and in clear water. If the sky is overcast or the water is murky, switch to hot colors such as chartreuse.

- Crappie often inhale a crankbait, then swim off to one side or the other. You won't always feel these hits, but you will notice the line moving sideways if you pay attention to your line at all times.

- When fishing deep-running crankbaits, try working your pole with a pump-and-drop action, pulling the pole forward and dropping it back. This allows the lure to "tread water," giving crappie a chance to catch up and inhale it.

When trolling a crankbait, mark your line with a waterproof marker when the lure attains the proper depth. Then stop at the same mark when you release the lure to fish again.

SECRET WEAPON: LIPLESS CRANKBAITS

All types of crankbaits can be used to catch crappie, but lipless crankbaits deserve further discussion because of their extreme versatility. Anglers can use them at all depths, in muddy water and clear, during all seasons and in almost any cover. Without changing lures, you can jig in deep-water timber, count down to crappie suspended by bridge pilings or buzz across the top of a brush pile. Best of all is their simplicity; anyone can fish these lures.

Lipless crankbaits go by a variety of names, including slab plugs, vibrators, rattlers, rattlebaits and sonics. The best-known model is the famous Rat-L-Trap made by Bill Lewis Lure Company. This wasn't the first such lure, but Lewis' Rat-L-Trap is so well known, its name is synonymous with lipless crankbaits. XCalibur, Strike King and Cotton Cordell are among the many manufacturers that also make popular lipless cranks.

Lipless crankbaits come in floating and sinking models, and in sizes ranging from tiny (1/10 ounce) to large (over 1 ounce). Smaller models—1 to 2-1/2 inches long, 1/10 to 1/2 ounce—work best on crappie because they're similar in size to the baitfish crappie feed on. Don't reject the larger sizes automatically, however. I've caught many crappie on bass-sized models, even though these don't take crappie with the regularity of shorter, lighter-weight lipless crankbaits more easily taken into the fish's mouth.

Each lipless crankbait has a line-tie eye on the back, which makes the lure run with its head angled down. Water pressure on the typically flat forehead produces a tight, convulsive shimmy that closely resembles a small baitfish zipping through the water. Crappie find this action irresistible.

Most models also contain sound-producing pellets. The lure's tight, fast vibration whips the pellets against the inside of the lure, creating a rattle that sometimes can be heard 50 feet from the boat. This clattering noise is especially

Lipless crankbaits are great crappie locators. The narrow body has little wind or water resistance, so you can cast long distances and retrieve rapidly, combing broad areas to find active biters.

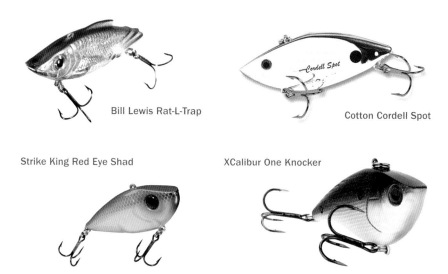

Bill Lewis Rat-L-Trap

Cotton Cordell Spot

Strike King Red Eye Shad

XCalibur One Knocker

important for enticing strikes in muddy water or dense cover, at night and on windy days.

Most anglers fish vibrators like other crankbaits, simply casting them out and reeling them back in, varying the retrieve speed and pausing occasionally. You also can fish them like bass jigs, casting the lure and letting it sink, giving it a good hard lift with the rod and reeling in the slack as it sinks again.

Vertical jigging is highly effective on summer and winter crappie suspended around deep ledges, weed lines, bridge pilings, sunken islands, bluffs and isolated brush piles. Position your boat directly over the target structure, then lower the lure until you feel it hit bottom. Engage your reel and take up slack. Then begin a delicate upward sweep of the rod tip to activate the vibrator. Move the rod tip as little as 12 inches or as much as 36 inches, experimenting as you fish to determine if the crappie have a preference. Then slowly drop the rod tip, letting the lure free-fall. Maneuver your boat around the structure, jigging the lure this way, and set the hook the instant you feel a hit. Strikes nearly always occur as the lure is spiraling downward, but most strikes go undetected until pressure is applied to the lure on the upward sweep.

A similar tactic is effective for fishing shallow sunken timber. Use a long jigging pole or fly rod to lower the lure near the structure—similar to a jig presentation, but give the lure considerably more action. Flicks of the wrist load a long rod, making the lure hop erratically. Watch your line carefully for any slackening or jerk that indicates a strike.

During the prespawn period in early spring, crappie begin following creek channels and other well-defined bottom structure toward their spawning areas. Anglers searching for them must cover lots of water, and lipless crankbaits are great

for this. Cast and retrieve them around staging areas such as secondary creek channels, outside creek bends and bottom channel junctures. Creek channels circling
humps or small ridges also are key spots.

As water temperature climbs, crappie move nearer to their spawning sites.
Cast for them on shallow flats close to deep water. When spawning activity is underway, most anglers stop using lipless crankbaits, putting them away until crappie leave
the beds and move back to deeper water. But they remain effective throughout this
season, especially where spawning beds are in more open water.

In late spring and early summer, try working your lures over the tops of
submerged weed-beds. If the vegetation is just a foot or two under the surface, many
anglers use a floating vibrator on 10-pound-test line. Retrieve with your rod tip low,
alternately reeling to draw the lure under the surface then pausing so it floats back
up. When the plants are deeper, use a sinking model and count it down to the top of
the vegetation before starting it back. Ideally, the lure should just tick the top of the
weed-bed on your retrieve. If it moves too fast over the weeds without hitting any, it's
not nearly as effective.

A sliding bobber presentation also works in this situation. Simply tie a small
vibrator beneath a slip bobber that's adjusted to place the lure just above the weeds.
Cast, let the lure settle, then jig, bringing the line through the bobber to make the
lure vibrate.

An excellent but seldom-used rig for tempting crappie holding on deep cover and structure is a
Carolina-rigged lipless crankbait.

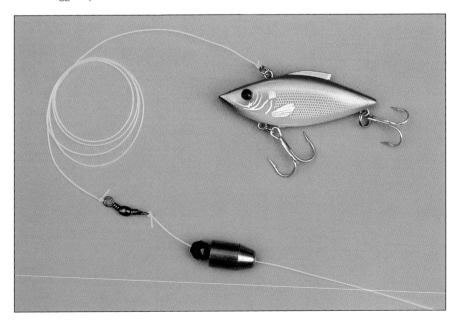

A few innovative crappie anglers are now using lipless crankbaits on Carolina rigs, a very effective technique when crappie are holding deep near bottom structure. Use a floating lure, a 1/2-ounce sinker and a 24-inch leader so you'll have good line control. With this rig, you can use almost any retrieve imaginable. The crankbait floats above the bottom, and each jerk makes the lure dive and swim erratically.

Versatility like this is what makes the lipless crankbait one of the best of all crappie lures. Every crappie angler should learn the many ways to fish this extraordinary bait.

LIPLESS CRANKBAIT TIPS

- For the best action, attach a lipless crankbait to your line with a loop knot or small O-ring, never with a snap swivel or heavy leader.
- The smallest lipless crankbaits work best with the lightest line needed for a particular fishing situation. In open water—around docks, bridge piers, outer edges of weed-beds, etc.—2- to 4-pound test is usually sufficient. When fishing around dense woody cover, 8-pound-test works well, although with some of the tiniest lures, the vibration may be somewhat compromised.
- A sensitive rod helps detect changes in vibration that could signal a strike or indicate the plug has fouled. Rods also should be stiff enough to activate the lure with the least amount of rod movement. A light 6-foot graphite spinning rod with a fairly stiff butt and a flexible tip works well.
- The size of a lipless crankbait is not usually an impediment to generating strikes from crappie, but the size of stock hooks may prevent successful hookups. On larger lipless crankbaits, replace larger hooks with size No. 6 to increase your catch.

Try to match a lipless crankbait's size to the size of the predominant baitfish. In late winter and early spring, for instance, larger lures like this Heddon Bayou Boogie may work better because small, young-of-the-year baitfish are not yet available. Switch to smaller lures in summer after baitfish spawn.

CATCHING CRAPPIE ON SPOONS

Few crappie anglers ever tie one on, but spoons are unexcelled when targeting prespawn and postspawn crappie on deep structure and cover. When properly pumped, cast, trolled or fluttered, these flashy metal lures wiggle like baitfish with the bends. Crappie are attracted by this action, and big catches of big panfish result.

Spoons include a big family of lures in many shapes, sizes, colors and weights. There are two primary groups, however: 1) casting and trolling spoons, which have curved bodies, and 2) jigging spoons, which generally have flatter, thicker bodies. Casting and trolling spoons typically are used when fishing open waters where hang-ups aren't a problem, but weedless versions are available that work well even in thick cover. Jigging spoons work best when fishing standing timber and other crappie cover that's best plumbed using a vertical technique.

You'll probably catch more crappie if you stick to 1/32- to 1/2-ounce spoons, which are easier for small-mouthed crappie to inhale. But whether a small or large version is best depends on various factors.

For example, when crappie in clear water are holding really deep—say 25 feet down—I opt for a heavier spoon such as the 3/8-ounce Cotton Cordell C.C. Spoon. This lure's weight gets it into the strike zone quicker, a big plus. For crappie on shallower features, I prefer a smaller spoon like the 1/12-ounce Acme Kastmaster. Crappie find it irresistible, and they're easier to hook on the smaller lure.

At one time, most spoons came in one color—silver. Today, spoons come in virtually every color, finish and combination imaginable.

Which color is best? There's no pat answer, but most anglers prefer silver, white and other light colors in clear water, and go with gold, red, orange, chartreuse or brighter colors and combinations in stained or muddy water.

Spoons also are available in realistic finishes resembling live baitfish. Crappie

Smart crappie anglers keep a variety of spoons in their tackle box. These lures are highly effective for catching America's favorite panfish on deep cover and structure.

BASIC TYPES OF SPOONS

1. CASTING/TROLLING
Mepps Little Wolf

2. WEEDLESS CASTING
Johnson Silver Minnow

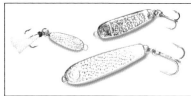

3. JIGGING
Cotton Cordell CC Spoons

feeding on shad are attracted by silvery, shad-like finishes. Where crappie feed largely on golden shiners, try a finish that mimics these baitfish, and so on.

Most spoons come prerigged with a split ring or snap swivel line-tie. Use it. Tying directly to the spoon is not desired as this inhibits the lure's action.

Most spoon-fishing strikes come as the lure falls and feel like faint taps or "heaviness" on the line. Using braided line allows easier detection of these subtle hits. Also, a fast-action rod may work better than medium- or slow-action rods typically used for crappie fishing because a too-limber rod decreases sensitivity and makes strike detection and hooksetting more difficult.

When crappie are holding in fairly shallow cover, another option is using a long jigging pole or fly rod to work the lure. Lower the spoon near cover and use flicks of the wrist to load the long pole, making the spoon hop erratically. Watch your line carefully for any slackening that indicates a strike.

Casting/trolling spoons, especially weedless versions, are great lures to use when searching for crappie around underwater creek and river channels, humps and other favored deep-water structures. Pull the spoon well behind the boat, maintaining a speed that allows the lure to rock gently back and forth without spinning. Adjust the amount of line until the spoon achieves the depth where you believe crappie are holding, then move slowly over good bottom structure while watching your sonar.

Non-weedless casting spoons can be difficult to fish around thick crappie cover, but they are applicable to open-water fishing situations where cover is sparse.

Casting spoons also work when retrieved across open horizontal structures such as submerged points or road beds. Throw the lure and let it sink, then reel up slack line. Next, rip the spoon off bottom by snapping the rod from a 10 o'clock position to 12 o'clock, then allow the spoon to flutter back to the bottom. Take up slack and repeat this process until the lure is beneath the boat. Be alert, and set the hook at any unnatural bump, wiggle or weightless feeling.

Jigging spoons do not work well as search lures. Instead, an angler should pinpoint fish first using electronics or other methods, then position the boat directly over them before using these lures. Bridge pilings, standing snags, ledges and other vertical structures may hold crappie that can be worked in this manner.

Present the jigging spoon using short, vertical hops. Lower the lure until it hits bottom or to a depth where crappie are suspending. Take up slack, sweep your rod tip upward 1 to 3 feet, then slowly drop the rod tip, letting the spoon free-fall but keeping "in touch" with the lure at all times. Repeat, and be attentive for pickups as the lure falls.

A guide on Missouri's Truman Lake gave me a refresher course on spoon fishing that's worth relating. We motored to a band of dead trees lining a river channel. "These trees look alike," he said. "But there's a fence corner that comes up to these two. It was inundated when the dam was closed, but a couple of cedar trees still stand there, and they attract lots of nice crappie."

I tied on a green-and-black jig as the guide instructed, but after fifteen minutes, no crappie had fallen for it. The blue-and-white jig on the guide's line also was ineffective.

"Maybe the crappie aren't here today," I suggested.

"On the contrary," he said. "Ninety times out of a hundred, I'll catch a dozen or more crappie in this spot. They're here. We have to figure out what they want."

Jigging spoons are available in a wide variety of colors and patterns. They often catch slabs when worked vertically over crappie-holding cover and structure.

Minnows drew no strikes, nor small spinners. But when the guide lowered a jigging spoon into the cedars, he hooked a slab. Over the next hour, spoons produced thirty fat crappie for us.

"Don't give up on a previously productive fishing spot too quick," the guide told me. "Sometimes crappie are persnickety; they want something different. That's when spoons often work."

Remember that next time you find crappie hard to catch.

SPOON TIPS

- When action is slow, make minor alterations to your spoon and see if the situation improves. For example, in muddy water, it's sometimes helpful to superglue an XCalibur rattle to the spoon as the added sound may help crappie zero in on your lure. If the spoon you're using has a plain treble, consider using a feather-dressed treble instead. A plastic tube or curlytail body can be added to the hook to change the action, texture and color, or you might tip the hook with a minnow or scent bait.

- If you feel hits but are unable to hook the fish, short strikers may be the problem. In this case, try adding a crappie-jig trailer behind the spoon. Tie a 6- to 8-inch piece of light mono to the spoon hook then add a 1/64- or 1/32-ounce crappie jig to the tag end. Or remove the spoon hook and tie the jig rig to the split ring. The smaller offering darting behind the larger spoon often entices wary crappie to strike.

- Some anglers like to remove the treble hook that comes on some spoons and replace it with a single hook that provides better hooksetting penetration and permits the release of more fish alive.

- Spoons often twist line. To combat this, use a high-quality ball-bearing swivel above a leader to which the spoon is tied, and if necessary use a snap swivel to attach the spoon.

- If you get snagged when working a spoon vertically in timber or other heavy cover, pull the line tight, then let the spoon drop. The weight of the spoon often pulls the hook free.

- Old, dull spoons can be given new shine by cleaning them with metal polish. If the tarnish is heavy, use a piece of fine steel wool first.

- For more variable action, try replacing the factory line-tie on a spoon with an XCalibur Tear Drop Split Ring. Tying to the narrow end of this ring will keep the spoon in a tight wiggle. The wide end allows for a wider wobbling action. At times, subtle variations such as these can make the difference between catching a lot of crappie or none.

- Savvy spoon fishermen use sensitive fish finders that allow seeing a spoon as it is fished around crappie beneath the boat. With good sonar, you can place the lure right on a persnickety crappie's nose and work it with various actions. Knowing you're in the strike zone reduces frustration, encouraging you to try various tricks until one produces the desired result—a crappie in the boat.

- When working a spoon around suspended crappie you've seen on your depth sounder, be sure to reel the lure up just above the fish, not below them. Crappie often look up for food but rarely look down.

When fishing for crappie in deep, dense cover such as timber, brush and weedbeds, you'll avoid snagging and catch more fish if you use a weedless spoon like this Johnson Silver Minnow.

FISHING WITH BLADEBAITS

L ike crankbaits and spoons, bladebaits are renegade lures often considered outcasts by crappie fishermen brought up on a strict diet of jigs and minnows. Nevertheless, bladebaits are proven crappie catchers with unique characteristics that make them applicable to special situations.

The Heddon Sonar was the first mass-marketed bladebait, circa 1959, followed a few years later by Cotton Cordell's Gay Blade. Both lures are constructed with a stamped metal blade shaped somewhat like a baitfish. This is sandwiched between pieces of lead that form the "head," with line-tie holes on the blade's top edge and holes for two treble hooks on the bottom.

Although this basic design is the starting point for all bladebaits, each manufacturer today (there are several) has created a bladebait unique in shape, size and weight distribution. For example, while the bodies on the Sonar and Gay Blade are both straight and sleek, the positions and contours of their heavy heads produce different actions. Luhr Jensen's Rat'lin Rippletail and Reef Runner's Cicada have proportionally wider bodies with wavy and cupped tails. Such variations give each lure a unique action.

Bladebaits originally came in one color, silver, and one finish, flat. They now come in gold, copper and brass base colors. Finishes can be flat, hammered or rippled. Painted finishes have been added, too, giving anglers many color choices. Some companies such as Northland Tackle now have bladebaits in photo-realistic finishes that look almost like real minnows.

When water is cold and crappie are deep, bladebaits can be hot. Snapped upward, they swim through the water and

A bladebait swimming through the water creates a pulsating vibration that imitates an injured baitfish. Slab crappie find these lures hard to resist.

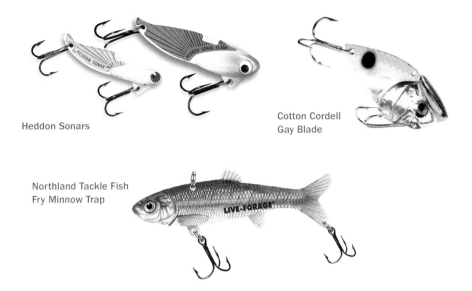

Heddon Sonars

Cotton Cordell
Gay Blade

Northland Tackle Fish
Fry Minnow Trap

create a pulsating vibration that mimics an injured or escaping baitfish. This attracts and allows a crappie to home in on the lure, especially when water is murky. You can vertically jig a bladebait to create a subtle swimming and fluttering motion, effective at attracting skittish, light-biting crappie; or retrieve it with occasional rips and runs to produce a dynamic, erratic action that might interest a slab in need of a wake-up call.

Bladebaits also are effective when targeting deep summer crappie on drop-offs and humps. When fishing drop-offs, keep your boat directly over the drop and cast to the top of the breakline, hopping the lure back to the boat. When fishing humps, position the boat off the hump and cast to the rise, working the bait on top first, then down the sides into deep water.

Most bladebait strikes occur on the fall. Watch your line closely and keep it tight during the retrieve.

Smaller bladebaits, 1/4 to 1/2 ounce, generally work best for crappie, but bigger models can produce where 2-pound-plus crappie are expected.

Some bladebaits have two or three holes on the top edge for line connection. Each placement allows for a different vibrating action, so read the manufacturer's instructions detailing which hole is most suitable for various applications. If there are two holes, generally the front one, with its tighter wiggling action and less vibration, is the best bet for vertical jigging. When three holes are available, choose the center one.

Never tie your line directly to a bladebait. One good smack from a crappie and the thin metal body will shear monofilament like thread. Use a round-bend snap or a split-ring to make the connection.

BLADEBAIT TIPS

- You can add noise to a bladebait's vibrations for even more crappie attraction. Visit a sewing craft shop and purchase stick-on eyes with little black plastic balls inside the eye dome, then add them to the head of each lure.
- Some anglers like to customize bladebaits by slightly adjusting the blades using pliers. Alter the blade so it is cupped or concave, and you'll create new action and vibration qualities, and change the descent speed.
- Use glitter nail polish to add a reflective color to bladebaits that looks like tiny scales.
- Most bladebaits have two treble hooks. A recent trend, however, is to replace these with two dual hooks. The hooks facing the center of the blade are removed. You can buy dual hooks or use wire cutters to snap off the third hook on each treble. Some anglers remove the forward treble altogether to reduce snagging.
- Scott Stecher of Reef Runner Fishing Lures likes to customize his company's crappie-catching Cicada bladebaits when action is slow. "I bite the head off a soft-plastic twistertail grub, leaving only two rings of plastic above the tail," he says. "Then I add this to the Cicada's rear hook. This addition slows the lure's fall and adds attractive color. Scent-impregnated grubs increase the effectiveness even more."

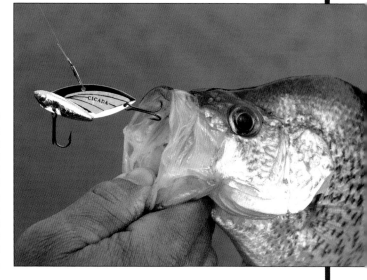

When fishing a bladebait, attach it to your line with a sturdy snap only, not a snap-swivel. If a snap-swivel is used, the lure's rear hook tends to foul on the line when the lure is sinking.

BAIT CONSIDERATIONS

CRAPPIE FISHING WITH MINNOWS

Minnows are an essential part of crappie fishing. Although adult crappie feed on other forage as well, small fish make up most of their diet. And because minnows can be raised commercially and are available at bait shops throughout the U.S., they're the bait of choice for many crappie anglers.

The word *minnow* often is used to describe any small, silvery fish. But technically, minnows are members of the family Cyprinidae, the largest fish family in North America. Some of the 200 species in the U.S., such as the grass carp and goldfish, grow very large. But most native groups such as shiners, daces and chubs seldom exceed 4 inches.

The species most used by crappie anglers are the golden shiner and fathead minnow, both produced by the ton on commercial fish farms. Arkansas leads the country in production, with some 6 billion minnows raised annually (61 percent of U.S. total). Sales information indicates golden shiners are most popular with anglers in the Southeast, Southwest and West, while fathead minnows are favorites in the Northeast and Midwest.

Farm-raised minnows aren't the only bait used by crappie fishermen. Many anglers catch wild baitfish with traps or nets. In fact, according to some estimates, about half of all baitfish are still caught from the wild. Species often used by crappie anglers include the bluntnose minnow, blacknose dace, creek chub, hornyhead chub, common and red shiner, and mudminnow.

Many regulations govern the use, collection and sale of minnows. These often are aimed at protecting waters from introductions of exotic species that could wreak havoc on an ecosystem. In some areas, only live minnows are prohibited. In others, minnows of any sort—live or dead—may be banned. Capture of wild fish is closely regulated in many areas as well. And if you catch baitfish to sell or use, you may need a special permit. Considering these things, it's important to study all regulations carefully before using minnows as bait.

For many anglers, catching crappie is most enjoyable and productive when fishing a live minnow under a bobber.

Golden shiner   ART BY Duane Raver, U.S. Fish and Wildlife Service

Fathead minnow   ART BY Duane Raver, U.S. Fish and Wildlife Service

Keeping Minnows Lively

In fishing, subtleties often make the difference between a good day or bad day on the water. Nowhere is this truer than when using live bait such as minnows. Sickly or dead minnows might work okay if you locate a school of super-aggressive crappie. Typically, however, sluggish, barely alive minnows won't catch as many crappie as frisky, healthy baits. It's important, therefore, to keep your minnows lively, something many crappie anglers find difficult to do.

Minnows purchased at a bait shop should be lively and without signs of stress or disease.

One important consideration is the hardiness of the minnows you use. Fathead minnows are hardier than golden shiners, for example, being better able to withstand drastic changes in water temperature, low oxygen levels and rough handling. Golden shiners, on the other hand, are hardier than emerald shiners. If you have a choice, use the hardiest varieties. (See sidebar below.)

HARDINESS GUIDE

Use this hardiness guide to select the best types of baitfish for your crappie fishing. The hardiest species are generally the liveliest on the hook.

- *Very Hardy*: fathead minnows, mudminnows, goldfish
- *Moderately Hardy*: young bluegills, creek chubs, hornyhead chubs, southern redbelly dace, blacknose dace, bluntnose minnows
- *Somewhat Hardy*: golden shiners, common shiners, red shiners, banded killifish
- *Least Hardy*: emerald shiners, small gizzard or threadfin shad, spottail shiners

It's also important to use healthy minnows, which have vibrant colors, unblemished skin and fins, and tend to cluster in the holding tank. Diseased minnows usually are much darker than healthy ones, often have damaged skin and fins, and tend to school more loosely, with individuals often swimming listlessly near the surface. Confine your purchases to shops that keep their bait in good condition. Sick minnows usually will die before you reach your destination.

After obtaining minnows, you must do several things to keep them lively.

First, avoid extreme temperatures and sudden temperature changes. A bag or bucket full of minnows placed on ice may be full of belly-up bait in minutes. Dumping minnows into water that is significantly warmer or colder also may cause sudden death. Temper the fish by allowing their water to warm or cool gradually. Slowly add small amounts of water from your storage container or the body of water you're fishing until the temperature regulates. Then keep the baitfish cool but not cold. A temperature between 50 and 65 degrees usually is optimum. High temperatures kill minnows as quickly as cold.

It's also best to use unchlorinated water. This can be obtained from the water you're fishing or from a well or rain water. If tap water must be added, let the water stand overnight so the chlorine evaporates or add dechlorinating tablets or drops. Additives also can be mixed with the water to keep ammonia and other harmful byproducts at acceptable levels.

Keeping the water well oxygenated is also important, especially if you need to keep the bait for more than a few hours. You can accomplish this using products made to assist in this regard, including aerators, trolling buckets and special livewells and tanks.

Finally, avoid overcrowding minnows, another cause of stress and death. Generally, one gallon of water will support 12 to 24 small to medium minnows. Minnows often are graded and sold by size, so take this into consideration when you make your purchase.

My method for keeping minnows lively is as follows.

First, I keep the minnows in the water my bait seller puts in the bags of minnows I buy. This water has chemicals that help keep the minnows lively.

Second, I ask the bait seller to add oxygen to each bag. Most bait shop operators can do this, and minnows will live much longer this way.

Third, I place the bag(s) of minnows in a Coleman Xtreme cooler that keeps ice for three days or more, even in 90-degree weather. Beforehand, I add a layer of crushed ice a couple inches thick to the bottom of the cooler, then cover the ice with a thick towel. The minnow bags are placed on top of the towel, the lid is shut and the temperature remains cool all day.

When I reach my fishing hole, I transfer the minnows and water from a bag into a Styrofoam minnow bucket. If I expect to be on the water all day, I sometimes use a

It's important for minnows to be kept cool so they remain lively. The author uses a Coleman Xtreme Cooler with a towel-covered layer of crushed ice on the bottom for this purpose. Minnows placed in the cooler in bags can be kept this way for up to a week, even during hot weather.

small battery-powered aerator to insure the minnows have adequate aeration. I keep the minnow bucket inside my cooler so the temperature remains optimum, and I open it to get a minnow from the bucket each time I need one.

Using this method, I've been able to keep minnows lively for several days.

Fishing with Minnows

Minnows can be fished using a variety of rigs and methods. They can be fished stationary or in motion under a cork. They can be tightlined. They can be trolled. They can be cast and retrieved. They can be used in combination with jigs. They can be rigged one at a time or in tandem. The ways in which you can employ minnows for crappie fishing are limited only by your imagination.

A few basic principles should be observed when making minnow-fishing rigs. For example, it's best to use a fine-wired, long-shanked hook that won't injure the minnow as much as a heavier hook. Such a hook also is more easily removed from the crappie's mouth. Several styles can be used, but Aberdeen hooks are traditional favorites. Pick a size that's appropriate for the size of minnow being used: No. 6 to No. 4 for small minnows, No. 3 to No. 1 for medium minnows, and up to 1/0 or 2/0 when using big minnows for trophy-class slabs.

Care should be used in hooking the minnow so it remains lively and stays on the hook. The lip-hook method probably works best overall and is done simply by running the hook upward through the bottom lip and then the top lip. This method is used primarily when the minnow will be pulled through the water, either when trolling or using a cast/retrieve presentation. However, it works quite well for still fishing, too, even though most crappie anglers still prefer hooking the minnow through the back, just behind the dorsal fin, when using stationary presentations. "Eye-hooking" (running the hook through the upper portion of the eye sockets) also is common but is more likely to kill the minnow.

Minnows typically are hooked near the dorsal fin for still fishing (left) and through the lips for trolling and casting (right). Light-wire hooks must be used to avoid killing the baitfish, and care should be taken not to pierce the minnow too deeply.

MINNOW TIPS

- Always keep the lid on your minnow bucket when fishing. Minnows remain less active if the top is on and the water remains cooler. As a result, you'll have more live minnows to use during your outing.
- When crappie seem persnickety, fish the outer edges of cover with no bobber on your rig. Without any weight except that of the hook and a small split shot, a minnow sinks very slowly, twisting and darting as it does. Crappie find such baits irresistible. You'll have to watch your line very closely as the bait sinks, looking for any slight movement indicating a hit. But when regular live bait tactics fail, this one can save the day.
- To fish minnows in and around wood cover, try this rig. Put a small bullet weight on your main line and tie a barrel swivel below it. Then tie a 4- to 6-inch leader (shorter leader in thicker brush) to the swivel, and a crappie hook to the leader. This rig is excellent for dropping a minnow through gnarly branches. The minnow doesn't have a lot of free line for swimming to nearby limbs. When the sinker hangs, a quick twitch pulls it off the limb. When the hook snags, the sinker can be lowered to pull the hook free.
- Clear, wide-mouth plastic jars that hold 2 pounds of nuts or candy work great for transporting live minnows without spilling.

Snipping off a small portion of a minnow's tail will cause the baitfish to swim erratically, making it more enticing to fish that might otherwise ignore your offerings.

MINNOW BUCKETS

Minnow buckets usually are made from metal, plastic, Styrofoam or a combination of these materials. Many anglers prefer metal or plastic buckets instead of Styrofoam because they are more durable. However, several Styrofoam buckets can be purchased for the price of a single metal or plastic bucket, and there's evidence that minnows may stay much livelier in a Styrofoam bucket.

In one of his books, *Advanced Crappie Secrets*, crappie researcher Steve Wunderle tells about experimenting with Styrofoam, plastic and metal minnow buckets to determine if minnows survived longer in one or another.

He found Styrofoam buckets superior for keeping minnows alive during late spring, summer and fall, largely because water in Styrofoam buckets stays cooler longer. In fact, none of the forty-eight minnows in the Styrofoam buckets Wunderle tested had died after eight hours, while half or more of the minnows perished in the other bucket types during the same time.

This is an extremely simplistic overview of Wunderle's experiment and results, which you should obtain and read. But it does point to the fact that Styrofoam minnow buckets may be better at keeping minnows frisky than buckets of plastic or metal throughout most of the year.

Today, anglers can buy plastic buckets with Styrofoam liners that provide both durability and temperature control. In hot weather, they're ideal for keeping minnows cool and lively. They work great for ice fishing, as well, because they have less of a tendency to split or crack than Styrofoam alone. The bucket's hard outer shell protects the foam inner liner.

Also available are trolling-style buckets that have a more hydrodynamic shape to pull easily through the water behind a boat or a wading angler. Most are made to float face-up for easy access to the bait, and each has small slits or openings that allow water to flow through and aerate the minnows. If you troll a lot, these are worthy of consideration.

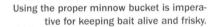

Using the proper minnow bucket is imperative for keeping bait alive and frisky.

ROSY RED MINNOWS

Rosy red minnows, sometimes called pink minnows, are an unusual color strain of the fathead minnow. The name comes from the baitfish's reddish-orange hue, which closely resembles that of an orange goldfish.

Rosy reds were first propagated by fish farmer Billy Bland of Taylor, Arkansas. In the early 1980s, Bland began noticing a few orange fish in loads of black fatheads bought for his aquaculture operation. He hand-picked these rosy reds, placed them in a special rearing pond and eventually established a breeding population. Soon, he was producing rosy reds in quantity.

Bland's first big market was the "feeder" market. Rosy reds replaced freshwater guppies as the food of choice for many predatory aquarium fish.

But before long, fishermen also heard about Bland's new minnow and coerced him to sell some for bait. Many of these anglers were crappie fishermen who knew that orange goldfish were relished by big slabs. They felt the rosy red's goldfish-like colors would also attract jumbo crappie.

They were right. Not only were rosy reds superb crappie bait, they frequently outproduced regular minnows. Bait dealers soon were inundated with orders for these newfangled minnows. The rosy reds' hardy nature made them especially popular with Northern ice fishermen. But other anglers were taking notice, too. Soon, rosy reds were available in thirty-three states.

Are rosy reds really better than golden shiners or other crappie minnows? Many anglers say yes.

Steve Filipek is an avid crappie fishermen and a fisheries biologist with the Arkansas Game and Fish Commission. He's been fishing with rosy reds for years. "My crappie catch has probably doubled since I started using them," he says. "I no longer feel comfortable using regular minnows."

Talk to those who use rosy reds, and you'll hear dozens of similar testimonials.

"Rosy reds have always been a very desirable bait species," says Mike Freeze, owner of Keo Fish Farms in Keo, Arkansas. "The primary downside to rosy reds, as far as fishermen are concerned, is cost. They're slightly more expensive because the average production of rosy reds on fish farms is not as great as the average production of other minnows. That extra cost is passed on to consumers.

"Rosies also may be more difficult to find because many bait dealers won't carry them," Freeze says. "Bait shops need another tank to keep them in, or they have to partition their bait tanks to hold the rosy reds. Most won't go to that expense unless the demand for rosy reds is great.

"On the good side, rosy reds are very hardy. They live longer than shiners in a minnow bucket or bait tank. And fishermen tell us if the water's not too muddy, they catch more fish on rosy reds than other minnows. If water conditions are such that prey fish are relying on sight to find their food, they'll home in on rosy reds much quicker because they can see them at a greater distance than other minnows."

Rosy red minnows have an orange
hue, almost like goldfish.

SECTION V

SEASONAL SAVVY

CRAPPIE FISHING DURING SPRING'S SPAWN

The rising sun shines brightly through the cypress trees as my son Josh and I slide a johnboat into the oxbow lake. I paddle while Josh ties a jig to the line on a long pole and slides into his waders. The boat serves merely to transport us from the ramp to shallows on the oxbow's far side. Today, we'll wade fish.

All conditions—water temperature, day length and other factors—must be perfect for us to succeed. And on this day, they are. We see crappie as soon as we start wading.

The water they are in is just inches deep. In most places, it's not deep enough to hide the crappies' dorsal fins. Even where it is, we can see swirls the fish make as they move in the shallows.

A flip of the line places Josh's jig beside one swirl. Immediately, a crappie nabs the lure. The jig pole arcs as Josh lifts the crappie, removes the hook and places the panfish in the fish basket tied to his waist.

I've chosen a different tactic—pitching a Blakemore Road Runner spinner rigged on an ultralight spinning outfit. This proves equally effective. I cast to one fin and get an immediate strike. It's a dandy fish. I quickly add it to my basket and make another cast with the Road Runner. I can see crappie in every direction.

After an hour of fishing, my fish basket is getting heavy. When I reach the boat, Josh is finishing his count. "Twenty-one, twenty-two, twenty-three . . . twenty-three crappie. Not too bad, huh?"

I had twenty-two.

Spring is a season of bounty for crappie anglers. When these panfish are in the shallows on their beds, it's often easy to catch dozens in a short time.

The Spring Invasion

Crappie invade shallow-water haunts along the banks of lakes, rivers and ponds during the spring spawning season. This makes them much easier to find and catch than during other seasons and results in more anglers fishing for crappie during this period.

Several spawning events help account for the good-luck days anglers experience in spring.

First, during the week or two just prior to the actual spawn, male and female crappie go through sort of a feeding frenzy to offset their reproductive growth spurt. They're also trying to add energy reserves for the stressful spawning period when activity increases. Consequently, crappie are feeding more, and this is a good time to catch fish.

Another fact in the angler's favor is the concentration of fish during the spawn. There may be dozens of nests in an area little bigger than a school bus. And there may be several beds this size along a 100-yard stretch of shoreline. Because crappie are holed up in the shallows, they're much simpler to find.

Male crappie vigorously defend their nests from egg predators or anything they perceive might be an egg eater. If an intruder gets too close, the defending male chases it, nipping and biting until it leaves the area.

Crappie anglers can turn this aggression into a fishing boon. Many crappie taken during this period strike the bait not because it represents a food item but because it has intruded into their nesting territory. Males protect the just-hatched fry and continue to fiercely attack anything that comes near the nest area. Therefore they remain unusually susceptible to baits and lures for a week or more after nesting activities end.

When and Where to Go

A clear understanding of factors that trigger crappie spawning is essential for successful spring fishing.

Water temperature is the primary key. Most experts quote a figure of 56 degrees as the temperature at which nesting activity begins. But spawning's peak may not occur until the temperature climbs to 58 or 60 degrees.

The exact time when the water reaches this temperature varies from year to year, latitude to latitude and one body of water to another. It is important, therefore, that crappie anglers determine when ideal spawning temperatures are

Michelle Sutton of Wynne, Arkansas, caught these nice crappie on their spawning bed in a shallow cove.

most likely to occur and do some on-the-water investigation that will lead to a visit during peak nesting time.

Looking at sunrise-sunset tables can be helpful. I learned this from Steve Wunderle, who wrote the excellent guide *New Techniques That Catch More Crappie*.

In this book, Steve tells of a study done on Missouri's Table Rock Lake by fisheries biologist Dr. Fred Vasey. Vasey learned that "the first [crappie] nests to appear had an average of 13.2 daylight hours," and "the last nesting sites occurred when the daylight averaged 14.6 hours." In other words, you can determine when spawning will begin and end, and therefore postulate when it might peak, by calculating the number of hours between sunrise and sunset on a given day.

Anglers also should remember that crappie almost invariably nest in shallow coves protected from wind and wave action. Finding areas with these characteristics is the key to finding crappie beds. Nests often are near a log or other large object over a bottom of sand, fine gravel or interwoven plant roots. The depth where nests are found can vary considerably, from less than 1 foot to as much as 20 feet. But most will be in 1 to 5 feet of water.

Additional Facts

Several nuances of the spawn may not be readily apparent. One is the fact that the biggest crappie often are in deeper water when smaller males are first preparing nest sites. For this reason, it's smart to try fishing deeper areas away from shallow-water beds, sometimes as deep as 7 to 15 feet.

Another fact to remember is that spawning activity is spread out over a period of time. Female crappie don't all lay eggs at the same time, and an individual female may deposit eggs in batches over a period of two weeks. This assures successful reproduction and provides anglers outstanding shallow-water fishing opportunities for an extended period.

If you've fished a body of water before, and you know where crappie beds were previously, return to those areas. Crappie nest in the same locales year after year.

You also can examine a bottom contour map to pinpoint hotspots. Look for underwater creek channels near shore. Crappie follow channels from deep water to shallow and disperse on both sides of the channel/spawning cover junction if conditions are suitable. Shallow water in backs of feeder-creek bays often proves good as well, as do migration corridors leading to shallow cover—stump rows, old fence lines, weed lines, ditches and the like. The key combination is shallow water with abundant cover and a firm, not silty, bottom.

Get Wet

To reach spring crappie in extreme shallows where a boat won't go, Grenada Lake, Mississippi, crappie guide Brandon Fulgham dons his waders and carefully makes his way along while jigging around big cypress trees. "When fishing lots of look-alike cypress trees, you have to remember not all trees are created equal," Fulgham says. "I look for big trees with lots of knees around them and long limbs overhanging the water. These usually produce more fish than smaller trees with fewer knees and branches. Fish slowly, and cover every angle of each cypress. And be sure to fish around underwater knees away from the trees as these often hold

big slabs. After catching a few fish, you'll start noticing a locational pattern and can fish specifically in those spots where crappie are holding that day."

Cork a Jig

Missouri crappie pros Travis and Charles Bunting like to work big jigs under slip corks for trophy spring crappie. "Using a slip cork provides added versatility when fishing jigs," Travis says. "It allows you to catch crappie on a falling lure, a moving lure or a motionless, suspended lure—whatever crappie prefer that day. When fishing clear water, the weight of the cork also allows you to cast to shallow crappie from a greater distance to avoid spooking fish."

The Buntings vary the size of the jighead and/or body to adjust the speed at which a jig falls. This triggers reaction bites. "For example, when fishing stained water, we may change from a 1-1/2-inch Southern Pro Stinger body to a 2-1/2-inch Southern Pro Walleye Tube," says Charles. "This slows the lure's fall and puts a bigger profile in the water that's easier for crappie to see."

Two-Handed Fishing

Learn to do it right, and you can almost double your spring catch by fishing with a pole in each hand like Lake Eufaula, Oklahoma, crappie guide Barry Morrow. "I use 10- or 11-foot poles with Tennessee handles and baitcasting reels," he says. "I hold the poles with my hands in front of the reels (reel upside down) and lace line between my first two fingers. The rod-handle butts rest on my

elbows, and I keep the rod tips about 2 inches above water. Detecting a bite is all about feeling the bite and the weight of your jigs. Set the hook like a mousetrap going off, and lift fish by raising your rod high and swinging the crappie into your boat."

Try a Road Runner

Greenville, Mississippi, crappie pro Brad Taylor uses a unique rig for nabbing slabs just after the spawn. "I put a 3/8-ounce egg sinker on my main line and loop the line through the weight four times," he says. "Then I tie a Blakemore Road Runner spinner 12 to 15 inches below the sinker and tip it with a lively minnow. This creates a deadly combination. I use 16-foot B'n'M poles to get these rigs as far out in front of the boat as I can. Then I push them along swiftly to cover as much water as I can and catch these scattered crappie. This tactic produces good numbers of fish, including some heavyweights."

Fish Cover Others Miss

When fishing for spring crappie in the shallows, most anglers simply move from one piece of visible cover to another, fishing each with a jig or minnow. But Brad Whitehead, a crappie pro who guides on Pickwick and Wilson lakes in Alabama, says it's important to watch for less-visible underwater cover as well. "In spring, I fish a heavier jig than most crappie fishermen, usually 1/4 ounce," he says. "This allows me to fish faster, dropping the jig beside underwater stumps and other cover, especially those on shallow points. I catch lots of big crappie this way because I'm fishing places most other anglers miss. That's where the real slabs often hide. When cold fronts hit, I switch to a cork and minnow rig. Both rigs help load the boat in spring."

Conclusion

There's no doubt about it: spring crappie fishing is the best there is. Anglers who fish their favorite waters this time of year will find it much easier to find and hook lots of these fun-to-catch panfish. And by applying the tips provided here, your catch rate should improve even more.

Don't miss out on the year's best action. Be on the water when crappie are on their beds and take advantage of this spring fishing bonanza.

PRO TIP

"It sounds crazy, but you may be able to smell areas where crappie are bedding. Nesting males exude an oil with a very distinctive odor. Zero in on these spots and your catch rate will soar."

—Todd Huckabee, www.toddhuckabee.com

RIVER TACTICS

R
ivers. Crappie. To most crappie anglers, these two words are totally unrelated. Crappie are considered lake fish, and when planning a crappie-fishing junket, rivers receive little attention.

If you were to live in a land of rivers and few lakes, however, you might think again about fishing flowing waters. Such was the case with Bill Peace of Jonesboro, Arkansas. Growing up in the lake-poor Delta of northeast Arkansas in the 1940s and '50s, Peace began his crappie-fishing career on big bottomland rivers like the Black, St. Francis and White. Today, there are several excellent crappie lakes near his home. But often as not, when it's crappie he's after, Peace returns to fish the rivers of his childhood.

"I started crappie fishing when I was just a boy," says Peace. "Back then, lakes were scarce in northeast Arkansas, so we fished the rivers. I discovered early on just how good river fishing can be, and though I often fish lakes nowadays, it's river fishing I enjoy most. It's a different, more challenging way of crappie fishing. But when it's good, it's the best there is. There are times when we catch fifty crappie an hour, and a lot of those will be big—one to three pounds each."

The best crappie rivers, according to Peace, are warm lowland rivers meandering through rich bottomland soils. If a river is cold enough for trout, or cool enough for smallmouth bass, it's not likely to hold many crappie, he notes. Bottomland rivers, on the other hand, often support phenomenal crappie populations.

Current and often-changing water conditions can make river fishing tough, but big lowland rivers often produce big stringers of crappie for anglers savvy to the ways of moving-water panfish.

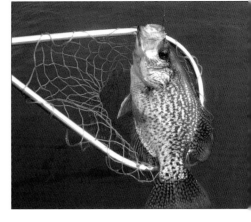

Fertile delta river systems often produce enormous crappie. During the spawn, most are caught from shallow backwaters and other areas where current is minimal.

"Some crappie fishermen never fish rivers," Peace says. "That's a big oversight. River fishing can be outstanding if you know how to do it."

Seasonal Considerations

River crappie are transients, moving from one area to another as seasons change. In summer and winter, extremes of heat and cold drive them to deep-water haunts, often in or near the main river channel. Spring and autumn offer more moderate water temperatures, allowing crappie to invade shallow, off-channel areas. During these seasons, they're often found in backwaters and other areas where current is inappreciable.

"If you know where to look for them, you can catch river crappie year-round," says Peace. "But the spring spawning season offers the best fishing. Crappie are in shallow areas then and easier to find. They're more aggressive than they will be during fall."

Pinpointing River Crappie

Crappie rarely spawn in the main channel of a river. Most make their nests in back-water areas out of the current.

"In spring, the best crappie fishing is in still waters off the main river," says Peace. "Look for big backwaters, side channels, places where current is reduced. Crappie prefer to spawn where they don't have to fight the current."

The areas Peace seeks have three important qualities: abundant cover, proper water temperature and stable water levels.

"River crappie usually nest where there's dense cover," he says. "Roughfish eat their eggs given the chance, so crappie get as far as they can back in brush tops, willows, stick-ups and other thick woody cover. When you're trying to find a good fishing area, start by looking for heavy cover in shallow areas off the main river.

"The second thing to look for is warm water," he continues. "Crappie begin spawning activities in water that's fifty-six degrees, and they'll move out of cooler water as soon as they can. The thing is, water temperature isn't the same everywhere in a river. It fluctuates from one spot to another, and that can make it tough to find fish. Crappie may move out of the main river and into a warmer tributary. Or they

The savvy river angler closely monitors changing water levels in the river being fishing. The rate of change often determines how good the crappie fishing will be.

may move to water that's a little muddier, because silty water warms quicker than clear water. It's important to find areas with the proper water temperature in order to find fish."

Fluctuating water levels also affect crappie behavior. And most big bottomland rivers are subject to extreme fluctuations during spring.

"Good river anglers keep track of changing water levels in the newspaper or through other sources," says Peace. "What you want to check is the rate of change. If a river is rising fast or falling fast, crappie fishing won't be good, even in backwater areas. The fish just quit biting. The best fishing is when there's a slow rate of change or no change at all, so try to plan your trip when the river's stable."

Establishing a Pattern

Being a successful river angler requires flexibility, Peace says. In other words, crappie anglers must be willing to change lures, tactics and locations as often as necessary to establish a fishing pattern.

"Lure color is a good example," Peace notes. "In the backwater areas I usually fish, crappie almost always hit a red jig with a chartreuse tail. If that doesn't work, a jig that's red-and-white or blue-and-white usually will.

"There are times, though, when my favorite colors just won't work. So I keep changing until I find something crappie will bite on that particular day under those particular conditions."

Anglers also may need to vary their presentation.

"You may have to raise and lower the jig as you're fishing," Peace says. "Or you may have to hold it completely still and watch for your line to go slack when a crappie hits. One day they like one presentation, the next day they may prefer another.

"The key to catching river crappie is establishing a pattern. Do they want jigs or minnows? If jigs, what color? Should I jig the lure or hold it stationary? Are they in willow thickets or brushy tops? We may be the best crappie fishermen in the world and go out and not catch a fish. On the same day at the same place, a novice may go out and load his boat with fish. The difference is, the novice was able to establish a pattern. You've got to find that pattern. That's the key."

Does Peace have favorite fishing spots on the rivers he fishes?

Willows growing away from the bank often hold schools of heavyweight river-system crappie.

"Everybody has favorite places to fish," he says. "I usually fish on the lower end of the White River, just above its confluence with the Mississippi. In that area, secondary willows are among the best crappie-fishing places. These are willows growing out into a backwater as the backwater silts in. The water moves up and then down, year after year, depositing more silt. And as the silt piles up, the willows take hold farther and farther out from the bank. Fishing the outermost willows in these areas can produce lots of big crappie.

"I'm continually on the lookout for new fishing areas, too," Peace continues. "When the water's high and muddy, and fishing isn't too good, I'll do some scouting. High water lets you get back into chutes, cuts and backwaters off the river, places you may not have noticed before. And while you're up in these areas, you may find that water off the main river is clearer and easier to fish. If you find the right spot, it could turn a bad fishing day into a good one. At the very least, you should find new places to try when water conditions are more favorable."

Is river fishing really that different than lake fishing? After reviewing Peace's suggestions, you may think not.

"The basics of crappie fishing are the same whether you're fishing a little lake or a big river," says Peace. "But fishing rivers and fishing lakes is teetotally different. You need to fish a river quite a bit to know exactly how and where to fish. You have to practice at it. River crappie are more aggressive because they've had to battle currents all their life. But they're more finicky, too, more likely to move around and change their behavior patterns. That makes river fishing tough.

"That doesn't mean you shouldn't try it, though. There have been times, especially during the spawn, when I've limited out in forty-five minutes. River crappie tend to gather in large schools in very small areas, and if you get on a pattern, you can tear them up.

"Lake fishing is fun in its own right," Peace concludes. "But if you want to experience the most exciting and most challenging form of crappie fishing, rivers are where it's at."

POSTSPAWN FISHING FOR RIVER CRAPPIE

After spawning, river crappie remain in off-channel areas until summer's heat warms the water to uncomfortable levels. As the temperature nears the 80-degree mark, crappie migrate back to cooler, oxygenated water in the main river channel.

"Catching summer crappie isn't hard," says Bill Peace. "But you must be able to pinpoint specific areas in the main river where crappie are likely to hold.

"Most crappie will be near current breaks like logs, willow thickets or rock wing dikes that have brushy cover around them. Fighting current is a waste of energy, so they try to find areas where current is reduced. You'll need to use bigger jigs in this situation and be prepared to get hung up some. Fishing in the current can be a lesson in frustration."

Peace suggests positioning your boat close to the structure you want to fish, then work the structure thoroughly. "A single spot may hold a dozen or more big slabs," he says. "Don't leave too soon."

SPRING FISHING TIPS

A lmost anyone can catch crappie when they're bedding in the shallows. The following tips, however, will improve your fishing success throughout the spring—before, during and after the spawn.

Watch the Weather

Successful prespawn anglers know how crappie react to changing weather patterns. This season has lots of bumps, starts and backups. Warming trends are interrupted by sudden cold fronts. Crappie migrate from deep water to shallow and back several times before settling into spawning patterns.

The best fishing usually is toward the end of warm spells. One clue is a cold front approaching after several warm days. During this time, male crappie start fanning in shallows. Females also move shallow, looking for food. Therefore, focus fishing efforts on shallow waters where spawning will occur.

When a cold front hits, crappie return to deeper waters, holding near distinct bottom structure where light penetration is minimal and winter cover is abundant. If conditions are sunny and windy (typical after a cold front arrives), wave action cuts light penetration, and crappie remain near mid-depth structure. Several days after the cold front hits, the wind calms, allowing greater light penetration and driving crappie to deeper structure and cover.

If weather remains sunny and begins warming before the passage of another cold front, crappie gradually begin migrating back to shallow waters. Rainy weather, especially a warm rain, sends them scurrying to shallow reaches.

Consider all these factors when selecting areas in which to focus your fishing efforts.

Try Tailwaters

Don't overlook the opportunity to take loads of spring crappie in the tailwater below a big-river dam. River crappie often move upstream in early spring, searching for spawning sites. When they reach a

When spring weather turns rainy, crappie often move from deep to shallow water, making them easier to find and catch.

dam, they mill around for a while, and you have an excellent chance for extraordinary catches. A jig/minnow combination often outproduces a jig or minnow alone in this situation. Cast around wing dams, boulders, lock walls and other current breaks where crappie can rest and feed.

Remember Hotspots

As crappie are caught and removed from a spawning bed, other fish move in to take over prime nesting sites. Therefore, fishing may continue to be good at a single site for many days throughout the spawn.

An Inconspicuous Marker

Crappie on beds often get spooked and disappear. If you wait 15 or 20 minutes and come back, chances are the fish will be in the same spot. But if you use an ordinary marker buoy to mark the spot, someone else is likely to see it and beat you to the punch. Instead, tie a piece of brightly colored yarn around a stick-up or weed stem near the bedding area. That way, only you will know the location of the hotspot.

Cut It Off

You're less likely to frighten skittish crappie if you turn off your outboard well before reaching the spot you want to fish. Drift into position, or use a trolling motor to cover the last few yards to your fishing area.

No Motor At All

In some situations, even the sound of a trolling motor can scare crappie off their nests. Avoid this by using a small paddle to scull your boat from the front seat. This is much quieter and may provide the edge you need to get closer. A cane pole or jigging pole is great for this style of fishing. If you're adept at sculling, you can keep on the move until crappie are found, fishing different spots all the while. And when employing one of the 10- to 20-foot featherweight poles now available, you can keep your distance to avoid spooking these edgy shallow-water fish.

Tilt your motor up and paddle to avoid spooking cagey spring crappie.

Go Weightless

If you're fishing with live minnows, and crappie seem especially watchful, don't weight your bait. Use a thin-wire Aberdeen hook on a 6-1/2 foot spinning rod matched with a long-spool, easy-cast reel full of 2- or 4-pound-test mono. With this rig, you can easily cast the unweighted minnow 50 feet or more. Hook the minnow through the back and cast toward likely hiding spots. The minnow should struggle near the surface for a short time, attracting nearby crappie. Then as the baitfish tires, it begins sinking, still wiggling enticingly. Crappie can't resist.

Slider Time

Any angler targeting spring crappie in dense cover also should consider fishing with Charlie Brewer Weedless Crappie Sliders. These unique lures are to crappie fishing what plastic worms are to bass fishing. When properly rigged, with the hook point of the special-made jighead buried in the grub, they can be worked through almost any cover without hang-ups. Cast and retrieve them around stumps and logs, work them like jigs in brush or fish them beneath a slip float in weed-bed pockets. There's simply no better snag-free lure for fishing spring hideaways.

A Little, Not a Lot

Jig/minnow combos are great spring crappie-catchers, too, but often too bulky for fishing tangles. You'll still have an edge, though, if you tip your jig with a tiny piece of minnow instead of the whole thing. The added smell/taste increases your catch when finicky crappie avoid plain jigs.

Plugs and Flies

Topwater plugs and flies don't make good crappie lures most of the year, but slabs in skinny spawning waters can see these lures more easily than fish in deeper water. Sponge-rubber spiders, popping bugs and little plugs such as Rebel's Bumble Bug and Big Ant make little disturbance when cast to bedding areas and often draw reaction strikes from fat male crappie guarding their nests.

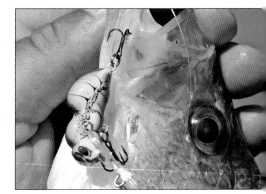

Tube Time

A float tube, or belly boat, provides a great means for slipping up on spring crappie in

Male crappie guarding nests often nab tiny plugs like Rebel's Big Ant.

backcountry oxbows, small ponds and other waters with no boat ramp. Or don some waders and go right in. An ultralight spinning rod and a few Crappie Sliders are all you need to nab slabs anywhere they hide.

Return to Deeper Water

Spawning may continue until the water temperature reaches 70 degrees or more. As soon as crappie leave their beds and shallow-water fishing takes a nosedive, look for fish in the same staging areas where they were found just prior to the spawn, places such as points, creek channel edges and drop-offs bordering shallow flats.

DOG DAYS FILLETS

I t was a typical "dog days" afternoon—fiery and humid with only an occasional breeze to bring relief. For several hours, bluegill fishing on the oxbow lake was outstanding. But as the chuck-will's-widows started their evening roundelay, the bream fishing tapered off.

Plop. The bobber twisted and settled. No takers. Move to the next spot. Plop, twist, settle. Wait. Still nothing. We maneuvered our crickets in, over, under, through and around every piece of cover, but no amount of wheedling could rouse another strike.

I decided a last-ditch effort for bass was in order. A barn swallow skimmed the water's surface as I tied the boat to a tall mid-lake snag. I'd seen two men sink a big cedar there two months earlier.

A baitcasting rod was put into play, and for the next 30 minutes, I plied the brush pile with a variety of lures. Nothing. Switching to an ultralight spinning combo, I tied on a tiny chartreuse tube jig, tipped it with a lively minnow and cast out near the sunken tree. Maybe the big guys wouldn't bite, but perhaps I could entice a couple of little ones.

The next hour was unforgettable. Not for the glorious rose-and-amber sunset that capped the day. Not even for the river otter I saw playing across the lake. On the first cast, I hooked a pound-and-a-half crappie, and there were twenty thrashing in the ice chest within the hour. None was a real "barn door," but several rated at least a "Wow!"

This fishing trip, and others like it, have convinced me to pursue crappie more often during summer. Granted, catching these feisty panfish isn't as easy in summer as during the spring spawn when crappie are concentrated in the shallows. But

Some crappie anglers quit fishing after crappie spawn, but summer is a season of plenty, too, if you know where to look for crappie and how to entice them.

for the angler who knows where, when and how, the rewards of summer crappie fishing are many.

The first rule of summer crappie fishing is keying in on deeper water areas outside the normal realm of shallow-water anglers. Despite the fact they're often moving, that's where most crappie hang out on a regular basis.

Concentrate your search in the 10- to 25-foot range. The clearer the water, the deeper you should look. Crappie are usually near woody cover along the edges of inundated stream channels, points and turns on weed edges, rock piles rising into well-oxygenated water, man-made fish attractors and other structure-oriented cover.

In waters with plentiful cover, the trick is finding the small percentage of it that holds fish. You may have to work hard to locate a concentration of crappie. Where cover is in short supply, a single sunken treetop may harbor dozens of slabs, but you must find that spot first.

Some deep-water crappie are found using hit-and-miss tactics like drift-fishing and trolling. But if you want to increase your hooking time and decrease your looking time, buy a good sonar fish finder with mapping software that shows major bottom features of the lake you're fishing. Electronic hardware is essential to find deep-water crappie consistently. Deep water, even water no deeper than the length of your boat, can hide a lot.

For example, it's one thing to know that a river channel zigzags through a long narrow cove. It's quite another to find a bend, ledge or some other nuance on the channel that will attract a school of crappie. Without sonar, you might never find such an area. But with a serious look at a bottom contour map and a quick check of prominent bottom changes with sonar, you could be catching slabs in minutes.

On lakes that stratify during summer, it's even easier to narrow down the

waters where crappie are found. Stratified lakes have a layer of cool, unoxygenated water on bottom and a layer of hot, oxygen-rich water on top. A layer of fairly cool, also oxygen-rich water called the thermocline is sandwiched between the two. Regardless of whether the thermocline is 8 inches thick or 8 feet thick, that's probably where you'll find crappie.

The depth of the thermocline varies from lake to lake. To find it, keep an eye on your sonar while moving around the lake, and look for suspended fish. You'll

A quality fish finder with GPS and/or mapping software is one of the angler's most important tools for pinpointing deep summer crappie.

Find summer crappie and you won't have to wait
long for a bite. Big catches of big fish often result.

notice most are about the same depth. That's the thermocline, or at least the depth zone, you're looking for.
When fishing, start at that depth.

If you don't have sonar, try drifting or trolling.
Rig your poles with minnows and/or different color
jigs set at different depths. Then use the wind or your
trolling motor to drift over prospective crappie-
holding areas. Make a large zigzagging sweep that
takes you past stump fields, weed edges and other types
of cover in fairly deep water.

When you catch a crappie, change your rigs to
conform to the fishes' bait and depth preferences, and
toss out a marker buoy to pinpoint the location.
Summer crappie are likely to congregate in fairly small
areas, and drifting a few yards either way could mean
getting out of the action.

A common mistake is staying in one place too long. In summer, if crappie are
present and feeding, they'll usually let you know right away. Contrary to popular
belief, the dog days are not a period of sluggishness. A high summer metabolic rate
means crappie are frequently feeding, and heavy schooling creates competitive group
activity. If you aren't catching fish within 15 minutes, try another spot.

Lightweight, sensitive fishing equipment is a must for light-biting summer
crappie. A good ultralight spinning outfit or graphite jigging pole works great if it has
a soft, sensitive tip. This allows you to lift up slightly and watch for the slightest bend
in the tip that indicates a fish has taken your bait. Watch your line for a slight twitch
or slackening that signals a hit.

Jigs and minnows, or jig/minnow combos, are the preferred baits of most
anglers, but don't overlook other possibilities. Small spoons, deep-diving crankbaits
and spinners also are productive. Four-pound line works well in most situations, but
you may want to switch to 6-pound or heavier when fishing heavy brush.

If you put your crappie pole in storage after the spawning season, get it out
again. Remember, summer crappie aren't hard to catch, they're just a little harder to
find. When you've zeroed in on a hot-weather slab hideout, likely as not you can stay
in one place and catch enough to feed your family—maybe enough to feed the next-
door neighbors, too. The dog days are crappie days, despite what you may hear.

PRO TIP

"Don't dismiss shallow water in summertime. A radio telemetry study on black crappie and white crappie discovered when water temperature rose into the eighties, many black crappie remained in their spawning coves in water as shallow as eight feet and did not move out to deeper water. White crappie also were nearby, suspended rather shallow on the main channel off deep-water ledges."

—Darryl Morris,
www.familyfishingtrips.com

CRAPPIE AT NIGHT

For many anglers, summer crappie fishing conjures up memories of the whip-poor-will's call and starlit nights. You can catch crappie during daylight hours this season, but your odds for success improve if you fish between dusk and dawn. During hot weather, many crappie work the late shift, and crappie anglers should, too.

Night-Fishing Logistics

The extent to which you are familiar with a lake and its crappie habitat is important when night fishing. If you search for good fishing spots in the darkness on an unfamiliar body of water, you could get lost, wind up on top of a stump or sandbar or something worse. Fish waters you already know or do some advance scouting during daylight hours. You'll catch more crappie if you can travel safely and directly to prime fishing locales you've previously identified and marked.

Putting waypoints in your GPS is helpful, and before fishing, you also may want to flag your fishing areas with marker buoys. The best places are near woody cover and provide crappie distinct travel routes from deep daytime haunts to shallower reaches used for night feeding. These include points, humps, creek channels, ledges and ridges. Lighted docks and marinas also are first-rate night-fishing spots.

Overhead lights draw baitfish and then crappie, and many dock owners place crappie-attracting brush piles nearby.

Ultralight spinning combos and graphite jigging poles with 4- to 8-pound line work great for night fishing. Jigs, live minnows and jig/minnow combos are the enticements preferred by most anglers, but small spoons and spinners also nab darkside slabs.

Get your fishing outfits rigged and ready to go before launching, and organize your tackle box, so you'll know where everything is. Be sure you have fully charged batteries for all your lights, and if necessary,

When summer temperatures peak, crappie often feed more actively at night, and anglers who plan their after-hours junkets properly may catch dozens of good-eating slabs.

Fishing from a lighted dock produced this nice mess of crappie for Arkansas anglers Josh Sutton (left) and Alex Hinson.

carry extra lantern fuel and mantles. You'll need anchors with an adequate length of rope to hold your boat stationary, marker buoys to pinpoint fishing holes and insect repellent to ward off mosquitoes.

Lights

If you go night fishing, you'll need lights, too—not just lights to see by, but specialty lights that draw crappie to your fishing hole. The latter work by attracting tiny animals called zooplankton, which attract baitfish such as shad and minnows, which in turn attract predator fish such as crappie. Crappie gather near or in the circle of light to feed. The angler drops in a bait or lure to catch them.

Early fishermen often used torches to illuminate the water when night fishing. Lanterns also have been used for decades, including the venerable Coleman lantern, a mainstay among many night fishermen even now.

One of the earliest specialty lights used for night fishing was a traditional floating model featuring a Styrofoam flotation ring surrounding a white, sealed-beam light similar to a vehicle headlight. This type of light, which includes products such as the Berkley Floating Light and Optronics' Floating Fish-N-Lite, is inexpensive and still widely available. Most run off 12-volt systems, with alligator clips attached to battery posts for power. The angler places the light (sometimes several lights) beside the boat where it floats with the beam of light pointing down to attract baitfish and crappie.

In recent years, floating lights with more energy-efficient LED or fluorescent illumination have become widely available. Also, green lights have become available in addition to white. Power for these models may come from standard 12-volt alligator clips, a cigarette-lighter plug or alkaline batteries. A molded handle on some of these units (Optronics' Floating Fish-N-Lite, for example) allows them

Many different types of crappie lights are available for the night fisherman. All can be helpful when fishing between dusk and dawn, but knowing how to use each correctly is necessary for success.

to double as spotlights, camp lights or boat lights. The best also have safety fuses and long, safely insulated cords. One innovative model, Optronics' model FLL-712UV Floating Fishing Light, has a built-in black light on top to help illuminate your line.

Also now available are submersible lights that slide beneath the surface and light up the depths. Battery-powered, 12-volt, LED and fluorescent models are available, with white or green lights.

Many submersible models are weighted internally or otherwise constructed so they sink immediately when put in the water. Berkley's Underwater Fish Light Rattle is such a light. Others such as Bass Pro Shops Submersible Fish Lights sink only after the addition of a weight to a swivel clip on one end of the light. These float when unweighted, so the user can vary where they are positioned in the water column for increased versatility.

Submersible lights that use fluorescent bulbs often are available in different lengths as well. Bass Pro's Submersible Fish Lights, for example, come in 9-inch and 21-inch sizes. Hydro Glow manufactures lights up to 4 feet long.

Fishing lights are available in two primary colors: white and green. You might wonder why red lights aren't used, or blue or purple. Why white and green? And which color is better? Does it really matter?

Darrell Keith, founder of Hydro Glow Fishing Lights in Dawsonville, Georgia, has spent years studying how lights attract fish. He said white and green wavelengths of light are most attractive to plankton. Plankton is a primary food of many baitfish, so when plankton gather in the lighted portion of the water, baitfish move in to enjoy the banquet. The baitfish in turn attract crappie and other gamefish looking for an easy meal.

"Plankton migrate to light for reproduction," said Keith. "And green has best ability to cause this to happen. White works, too, but white light is absorbed very quickly in water. It doesn't penetrate very deep so it's less effective than green, which maintains its color character at much greater depths."

In some experiments, Keith put five different colors of lights in the water at the same time, and green always attracted bait (and thus sportfish) far better. This fact is common knowledge now among manufacturers of fishing lights, so green lights have quickly become most prevalent. White lights are still available and still effective to some extent, but not as effective as green. So when you have a choice, purchasing green lights probably is the best option. And if you still have white lights you use, adding one or more green lights will increase the effectiveness of your illumination efforts.

Fishing

When you arrive at your fishing spot, anchor or otherwise secure your boat so you can fish over primary structure and cover. Then position your lights on one side of

Lights done right: fishing around green lights suspended above a bridge channel produced this stringer full of plump summer crappie.

the boat and turn them on to illuminate your fishing area. Floating and submersible lights can be used separately or in combination, but combinations—a pair of floating lights positioned above two submersible lights, for example—tend to be more versatile, lighting multiple levels of the water column to attract crappie no matter where they are, while also providing more above-the-water lighting for tying knots, hooking bait and unhooking fish.

You can start fishing immediately, but bear in mind that crappie probably won't show up until baitfish appear. This may take anywhere from five minutes to an hour or more. So relax, have a soda and chew the fat. If you've chosen a good fishing area, you'll soon notice baitfish around the light. At first there may be only a few, but where shad and minnows are plentiful, a whirling mass of small fish soon will be swimming in the lighted water. If the water is clear enough, you may actually see crappie running through the schools of baitfish and picking them off.

These crappie can be caught in many ways. A weighted live minnow beneath a slip cork is a good enticement, and jigs the size of the predominant baitfish almost always prove productive. Some anglers like casting and retrieving spinners through the circle of light; others prefer working jigging spoons directly beneath the boat.

If crappie are feeding on shad attracted to your lights, shad may outproduce minnows. Where legal, catch them with a dip net or cast net, then clip the tail or fins to give them an erratic, "crippled" action. Crappie can't resist.

Swarms of mayflies may be attracted to your lights as well. And at times, crappie gorge on the mayflies while refusing baitfish. Be watchful for such phenomena and act accordingly.

At times, the best fishing is within the circle of illumination created by your lights, but on some nights, you'll catch more crappie by fishing dark water at the edges of light. This may indicate there's structure near the place they're biting and none where there's no action. Moving the lights or boat to get positioned more directly over the fish may help.

Determining the proper depth to fish is perhaps the biggest challenge. If the lake is clear, crappie may be at 15 to 30 feet, sometimes more; in stained water, 5 to 15 feet; and in muddy water, typically less than 5 feet. The key to success is presenting your bait at the level where fish are feeding, but not too far beneath or above the strike zone.

Targeting crappie after dark provides lots of time to sit and socialize with your fishing buddies. Anglers of all ages enjoy the thrills, the laughs and, most of all, the companionship an after-hours crappie junket provides.

So give night-fishing a try this season. There's no better way to catch crappie when the heat is on.

SAFETY FIRST

When crappie fishing at night, always follow these safety precautions:

- Be sure your boat is outfitted with proper navigation lights, all of which are in working order.
- Carry a spotlight or flashlight so you can watch for obstacles and signal your presence if another boat approaches.
- Operate your boat at a slower speed and watch for the lights of other vessels.
- Wear a lifejacket and kill-switch at all times.
- Let a friend or relative know where you plan to fish and when you plan to return.

BLACK LIGHTS

Black (ultraviolet) lights are useful night-fishing aids. They illuminate fluorescent monofilament, making it more visible over a greater distance. When the ultraviolet lights are on, you can keep an eye on your line and watch for the slightest twitch or movement indicating a bite. Rods with fluorescent tips also glow brightly under black lights. And a dab of fluorescent paint on frequently used tools and tackle will glow, too, so the items are more easily found when you need them.

Most black lights run off a 12-volt electrical system or several D-cell batteries. Higher-end models often have features like the addition of green and/or white lights that can be used while rigging, cleaning or performing other general topside tasks; switches that allow you to turn on just the number of lights needed; and cordless, rechargeable construction that allows you to charge the unit at home with a 110-volt charger. Many have suction-cup feet for temporary rail mounting, and a few come with plug-in jacks that can be permanently installed on boat rails for easy on-off use.

SUMMER FISHING TIPS

During hot weather, crappie fishing gets tough . . . unless you know the secrets for summer success. These tips could help.

Try Bottom Fishing

When you know the thermocline's depth, look for areas where crappie-attracting structure covers the bottom at that depth, then bottom-fish a live minnow. Thread a slip sinker on your line, and below it, tie on a barrel swivel. To the swivel's lower eye, tie a 3-foot leader of light line tipped with a crappie hook. Add a minnow, then cast the rig and allow it to settle to the bottom. When a crappie takes the bait, the line moves freely through the sinker with no resistance to alert fish to a possible threat.

Pumping Iron

Summer crappie often suspend in 10 to 20 feet of water around the branches of standing submerged trees. To reach them quickly, lower a small jigging spoon on a tight line directly down through the branches. Give the spoon a short upward pull at every 3 feet of depth. Crappie often inhale the lure as it falls, and you won't know one is on until you raise your rod tip.

Attract Minnows, Attract Crappie

When fishing is slow during daylight hours, try an approach that duplicates the use of a crappie light at night. A light attracts insects, which in turn attracts minnows. But minnows also are attracted by chumming with dry dog food, bread crumbs or similar offerings. Scatter the chum by handfuls in several shallow-water areas, then move back to the first place you put chum and drop in a minnow. Fish each consecutive spot and see if your catch rate doesn't improve. Often, it will.

Scale Drop

Here's another "chumming" method to try when fishing is slow. Save some scales from the next crappie you fillet. Rinse them and store inside a sealable container

Spoons can be used to catch crappie year-round, but they're particularly effective in summer for taking crappie suspended deep around standing timber.

Hot-weather crappie often hide in the confines of dark cypress hollows.

filled with water. Carry the container on your outings, and if things get slow, drop a few scales in the water above inundated cover. Crappie blow out the scales of baitfish as they eat them. As the scales fall, they flicker and catch the eye of crappie, which often will move toward them to investigate. A jig or minnow presented on a tight line in the vicinity of scales you drop may get hit.

Cypress-Water Tips

Cypress-shrouded lakes and bayous tend to be shallow, which allows the water to reach excessively high summer temperatures. When the temperature exceeds their comfort level, crappie get lethargic and tough to catch. There's one place, however, where crappie still find comfort—inside hollow cypress trees.

The best trees have small to medium openings to the interior, thus excluding most outside light. Don't drop a minnow or jig inside the tree, but dangle it enticingly just outside the opening. Crappie will dart out when they see your offering, then usually rush back inside. Use heavy line, set the hook quickly and try to keep the fish outside the hollow so it doesn't tangle you.

Side-trolling

When trolling for summer crappie, try positioning your trolling motor(s) so they pull your boat sideways. This allows you to move in a very slow, controlled fashion so you can mine deep structures more efficiently.

Fish Storm Fronts

Summer weather tends to be stable, with minimal effects on crappie activity. But when conditions are such that afternoon thunderstorms are popping up day after day, plan an outing that allows you to fish just before a storm hits. Don't be on the water during periods of lightning or high wind. But if you can do it safely, be fishing when the clouds start to thicken and the wind picks up. Just before a storm hits, crappie often move to surface strata and feed actively. The action may last only a few minutes, but during those few minutes, you may catch more fish than you will the rest of the day.

Drop baits like Mann's Little George sink fast to quickly reach deep summer crappie.

After the Storm

When a summer storm ends, look for crappie in the thickest available cover—buckbrush, willow thickets, etc. Allow the wind to blow your boat against the cover. Use a long pole to work a jig into the brush, then fish little pockets most folks miss. Fish the jig with little movement, and work each hole thoroughly.

Drop a Drop Bait

A great lure for jumbo summer crappie is a tailspinner like Mann's Little George or Strike King's Sand Blaster. These often are referred to as "drop baits" because they sink very quickly. They're ideal for catching crappie on deep channel drops, humps and ledges. Freeline the lure to the depth where fish show up on your sonar, then retrieve it at a fast clip for hard reaction strikes.

Dock-walking

On bright sunny days, crappie may move fairly shallow if they can find overhead cover that shades them from bright rays. Boat docks, fishing piers and swimming platforms provide such cover, but anglers in boats may fail to get bites because crappie can see them. These same fish may bite, however, when the angler walks on the wooden structure and fishes from above. Crappie get used to foot traffic on these structures and seldom spook, so the quiet overhead approach often works when a bait presented from a boat won't. Let the wind drift a minnow or jig suspended under a bobber into the shade beneath the structure. Or try fishing a small jig vertically through wide cracks in boards over the shadiest water.

Slingshotting

Slingshotting, also called shooting, is another way to get at summer crappie hiding beneath man-made structures such as docks, piers and boathouses. This technique uses a short fishing rod like a slingshot to catapult a crappie jig into the shady area beneath the structure.

Use a 4-1/2- to 5-1/2-foot, medium-action rod outfitted with a spincasting reel or an autocast spinning reel that allows you to pick up the line and flip the bail at the same time. A 1/32-ounce jig is right for most situations, and you're better off using solid-body jigs when slingshotting because they stay on better than tube jigs. Pinch the jig carefully between the thumb and index finger of your free hand, pull the rod back like a bow, and aim and release the lure, letting it fly beneath the structure. With some practice, you can slingshot a small jig 15 to 20 feet under a dock or boathouse where big crappie are hiding.

Prepare for a strike as the lure falls. It helps to use highly visible line so you can see slight line movements that signal a taker. No hits? A slow retrieve close to the bottom frequently produces.

Care for Your Catch

Summer crappie placed in a stale livewell or on a stringer in hot surface water soon die and become soggy. For good-eating fish, take along an ice chest containing several inches of cracked ice. Drain melted ice frequently to prevent your fish from sitting in water. The result is firm, fresh fillets that have the delicate, delicious flavor for which crappie are famous.

For the best eating, place crappie on ice to keep them fresh.

FINDING AND CATCHING FALL CRAPPIE

Autumn fishing frustrates many crappie anglers. During fall, America's favorite panfish often are scattered and hard to find. Crappie may be deep one day, shallow the next and suspended at mid-depths the next. Fish may feed ravenously in the morning and get a bad case of lockjaw in the afternoon.

In lakes and reservoirs, summer crappie usually stay in or near the thermocline. Shallow-water action might be good during cool, low-light periods, but crappie rarely venture to the "dead zone" below the thermocline. For this reason, pinpointing schools of summer fish is relatively simple; find the cool, oxygen-rich water that forms the thermocline, and you'll find crappie.

This changes when fall begins. Cool weather begins lowering the surface water temperature. As the upper layer cools, it becomes heavier and sinks. This action forces warmer, lighter water below back to the surface. This water subsequently is cooled, just as the previous surface layer was, and descends as it cools. This mixing or "turnover" continues several weeks until the thermocline disappears, and all water in the lake is roughly the same temperature. This mixing effect also replenishes oxygen in deep water.

The end result is that fish formerly restricted to narrow bands of acceptable oxygen and temperature no longer are limited in their movements. Crappie once barred from the coolest depths because of low oxygen levels now may roam freely to

In water discolored by turnover, crappie usually hold tight to cover, so anglers should present baits and lures very close to cover objects such as stick-ups and stumps.

much deeper water. Likewise, where once fish could not spend extended periods in extreme shallows due to high temperatures and low oxygen levels, after turnover even these areas are acceptable. Crappie may now be found deep, shallow or anywhere in between.

Some waters don't experience turnover because they don't stratify in summer. Rivers are a case in point. So are many large, shallow, windswept lakes and some reservoirs with lock-and-dam facilities or hydroelectric generators.

In waters where fall turnover does occur, however, the angler will need to dig deep into his or her bag of tricks to zero in on schools of crappie. And it never hurts to have a few new tricks in your bag. Here are some that could help.

Find the Comfort Zones

The secret to crappie-fishing success regardless of the season is realizing that crappie always concentrate in areas providing the most comfortable living conditions and learning to identify those areas. In fall, conditions are theoretically such that crappie can live anywhere within a lake. In actuality, factors such as oxygen content, light penetration and food availability still greatly influence a crappie's choice of living quarters.

Consider, for example, all the debris and poorly oxygenated water being pushed upwards from the lake bed when turnover begins temporarily "trashes" the whole system. Crappie respond by seeking areas with better water quality. To find them, savvy anglers do likewise. An easy way is working tributaries bringing fresh water into the lake. Another way is looking for areas where turnover has not begun. On some large reservoirs, different arms turn over at different times; anglers can concentrate their efforts in areas not visibly affected.

When turnover causes excessive amounts of decaying debris to circulate in the water column, sudden significant drops in oxygen can result. When this happens, crappie must find oxygenated water immediately. They frequently solve the problem by going directly to the nearest source, which is surface aeration from wind and waves. Consequently, windswept shorelines with shallow cover may be productive crappie fishing spots.

Your first order of business when fishing during the turnover period should be finding comfort zones such as those just described and working them systematically to pinpoint crappie. The following tips from veteran crappie anglers may help.

Dealing with Cold Fronts

Passing cold fronts are a common fall phenomenon. And when a front moves in, the fishing can quickly turn sour. Crappie still can be caught, however, if the angler knows how to deal with this situation.

To catch crappie after a fall cold front passes through, Kentucky crappie guide Steve McCadams recommends fishing downsized lures near cover with a slow vertical presentation.

"Anglers can't control the weather," says Kentucky crappie guide Steve McCadams. "But they can adjust their presentation and be more effective in catching crappie when weather patterns turn nasty. I've seen crappie have a drastic mood swing literally overnight when cold fronts descend, lowering surface temperatures with bone-chilling winds. After the front passes, high skies with a high-pressure system alter the crappies' feeding habits, too."

Crappie relate close to structure in this scenario, says McCadams.

"To catch them, you must slow down your presentation to a vertical style, keeping the bait in front of the fish longer and in their specific depth range," he notes. "Don't expect the fish to be aggressive and chase down a moving bait because they're holding tight on structure. Light or small lure sizes will help, too, as will using a bobber for slow, sinking presentations that assist you in keeping the bait in the strike zone longer."

Shooting Pontoons

Early-fall fishing can be extra-tough on the northern canal lakes frequented by fishermen such as Russ Bailey, a pro angler/crappie guide from St. Marys, Ohio, who

Ohio angler Russ Bailey nabs fall crappie by "shooting" Road Runner spinners under pontoon boats.

hosts the *Midwest Crappie* television series. These waters, built in the 1800s to support canal systems, are shallow and bowl-shaped, with little natural cover and no drop-offs, ledges or channels to which transition crappie normally relate. Although they're often brimming with slabs, fishing them presents special challenges.

"Shooting pontoons [a type of boat also known as a party barge] is my favorite technique on these lakes during the fall transition period," says Bailey. "Pontoon boats provide shade attractive to crappie that have started moving back into the shallows. To catch these fish, I use B'n'M Poles' 5-1/2-foot Sharpshooter rod and a spinning reel spooled with 6-pound-test Hi-Vis Yellow Sufix line. My lure is a 1/32-ounce Blakemore Road Runner head with a Hot Grub body by Southern Pro Lures."

Shooting requires practice to perfect but is easy to learn, Bailey says. The angler pinches the lure carefully, pulls the rod back like a bow, and aims and releases, letting the lure fly beneath the structure.

"Most pontoons are situated with their front against the sea walls," says Bailey. "This leaves the back of the pontoon area for you to shoot under. Shoot as far under the pontoon as possible. If you only get a couple of feet back, you may catch a few crappie but not as many as you could.

"After you shoot the jig, allow it to fall and watch your line closely," he continues. "You'll usually see line movement before you feel a strike because most fish strike as the lure drops. If the line jumps or moves, set the hook immediately. If you don't get a strike during the fall, use a slow, steady retrieve. The Road Runner blade and Hot Grub tail are hard for crappie to resist. It's common to catch ten to twenty fish under one pontoon."

Find the Baitfish

Fishing with his cousin and angling partner Coy Sipes, pro crappie angler Gil Sipes of Moody, Alabama, has won just about every national and regional crappie tournament there is. He says when Team Sipes fishes for fall crappie, they usually start by finding baitfish.

"Crappie usually will be with baitfish such as small shad, especially during the summer-to-autumn transition period," he says. "As nights get cooler, baitfish move shallower, often into water just 8 to 10 feet deep. To find them, be on a lake at dawn

Pro anglers Gil (left) and Coy Sipes troll Road Runner/minnow combos through schools of shad to nail big fall crappie.

and look for shad flickering and schooling on top of the water. When you find bait-fish, you can troll in that area to catch crappie with them."

The Sipes duo trolls with eight B'n'M Pro Staff trolling rods, each with a tandem rig using both live bait and a lure. On top is tied a No. 1, Blood-Red Tru-Turn Aberdeen hook baited with a live minnow. Two feet below this is tied a Blakemore Road Runner spinner.

"When we find the shad, we troll through the area with these rigs, adjusting the depth of the lures as the sun rises," Sipes says. "Before the sun is up, we keep the rigs shallower because feeding crappie will be right under the baitfish, which are at the surface. When the sun rises above the horizon, both the baitfish and crappie leave the surface and move deeper, so we adjust the depth of the rigs so they're deeper, too. This way, we can stay on crappie throughout early morning and enjoy good fishing even during this tough time of year."

Try Standing Timber

When turnover ends and the water starts to clear, crappie often concentrate around standing timber. Here the fish can move shallow or deep as water and weather conditions dictate. On cloudy or windy days when light doesn't penetrate very far into the

Catching big crappie like this has helped crappie pro Kevin Rogers win lots of tournaments, and often as not, in fall, he catches these slabs while working jigs around standing timber.

water, crappie may be within a few feet of the surface. Bright, sunny, post-frontal days may find them hugging the bottom. Adjust your tactics accordingly.

"When fishing standing timber, fish each tree for only a couple of seconds," says Missouri pro Kevin Rogers whose specialty is jigging vertical timber. "If you don't get a bite, move to the next tree. Too many people make the mistake of sitting or tying up to a tree. You'll catch more fish by using your trolling motor and moving from tree to tree."

Rogers has used such tactics to qualify for the Crappie USA Classic during six consecutive years. The way you present your lure, he says, is important.

"When vertical jigging around standing timber, after your lure reaches the bottom, grab the line with your free hand and gently raise the lure up the tree," he says. "Crappie will not go down to hit your bait so raising the lure puts the bait in their face. They can't stand it."

The transition from summer to autumn is jolting for both fish and fishermen. Crappie find their once secure world literally turned over on them. Anglers who fish these waters find their quarry more unpredictable than ever. Overcoming this seasonal nemesis will require all the skill, knowledge and patience you can muster. But when you finally zero in on a big school of hefty autumn crappie, you're sure to agree that the rewards make the extra effort worthwhile.

RIVER FISHING IN FALL

Because rivers are unaffected by turnover, they provide an excellent alternative for anglers dealing with "turnover turmoil" in fall. In summer, high temperatures drive river crappie to deep-water haunts, usually in or near the main river channel. Autumn offers more moderate water temperatures, allowing crappie to reinvade shallow, off-channel areas where they were found during the spring spawn. They're often in backwaters, river-connected oxbows and other areas where current is low. Because the water in these areas is shallower, crappie are easier to find, too. And they're more aggressive than they were in summer.

During the late weeks of summer and early weeks of fall, look for river crappie near wing dikes, logjams, willow thickets and other current-breaking structure in or near the main body of the river. As temperatures drop and autumn gets in full swing, look for them near willows, cypress trees and other woody cover off the main river in oxbows and backwaters. As autumn turns to winter, look for crappie moving back to deep-water haunts near the main river channel.

PRO TIP

"During autumn, crappie schools often hunt shad on big flats. On breezy days, I catch them by 'sailing,' placing sixteen 8- to 16-foot B'n'M rods in Driftmaster T-Bar holders and letting the wind blow me across these flats.

My reels are spooled with 8-pound Berkley Trilene 100-percent Fluorocarbon, and my lures—1/8- to 1/16-ounce leadheads with Road Runner bodies—are set from 8 to 15 feet deep until I determine the depth where crappie are feeding. As I drift, I use a Humminbird 787 sonar/GPS combo to mark my path. This allows me to retrace a path when I start catching crappie, using my trolling motor to keep me on course. If it's extremely windy, I put out one or two MinnKota drift socks to slow the boat to 1.6 mph or slower. This is one of the best ways I know to find and catch crappie this time of year."

—Jim Duckworth,
www.jimduckworth.com

STUMP BUMPING FOR AUTUMN SLABS

L ake Conway in central Arkansas has the distinction of being the largest lake ever constructed by a state game-and-fish agency. This sprawling impoundment, 25 miles west of Little Rock on Interstate 40, covers 6,700 acres. And while its size is impressive for a state-owned lake, the lake's dimensions are not its only distinction. Conway also is one of the stumpiest lakes in the country.

When the Arkansas Game and Fish Commission impounded Palarm Creek to create Lake Conway in 1948, it flooded a huge area of standing and cut-over timber. The result was a lake chock-full of dense woody cover, a lake boaters must still travel at a snail's pace if they want to keep from getting high-centered on a stump and avoid knocking the lower unit off their outboard.

The stumps, logs and snags in Lake Conway also created a haven for crappie. America's favorite panfish are extraordinarily plentiful here and often tip the scales at 1-1/2 to 2 pounds, sometimes more. They find the habitat quite to their liking, and being abundant, they are among Conway's most targeted species of sportfish. Folks come from throughout the country to enjoy the lake's excellent crappie fishing.

When using their "stump bumping" tactic, Arkansas crappie anglers Chris Mullins (left) and Ricky Lucius arrange eight poles in holders on the bow of their boat. They then use a trolling motor to maneuver the boat close to visible or underwater stumps so the rigs they are fishing actually bump against the cover to entice nearby fish.

I tell you all this because when Arkansas crappie pros Chris Mullins of Joiner and Ricky Lucius of Wilson told me about "stump bumping," a great crappie-fishing tactic they use to find autumn's often-scattered schools of slabs, I wanted them to demonstrate the technique on a body of water where they'd be put to the test. Lake Conway was perfect: stumps are everywhere, and fall crappie get so scattered in this abundant cover, they often thwart anglers' attempts to catch them.

So it was, Mullins, Lucius and I met at Lake Conway, and these two expert anglers demonstrated how stump bumping works.

"Stump bumping is a tactic that can be used any time of year," said Lucius as we motored to our first fishing spot. "But it's especially effective in fall. This time of year, crappie tend to stay closer to cover, and the rig we use for stump bumping lets you fish right against the cover so you're more likely to catch them."

"This rig also puts bait at two different depths so you can more quickly determine at which depth the fish are biting," Mullins added. "That's a big advantage for the fall angler."

The Stump-Bumper Rig

The key to successful stump bumping is using the special rig Lucius and Mullins employ. In basic terms, it's a double-leader rig weighted in such a way that one lure can be presented on or very near the bottom and the other lure is presented about

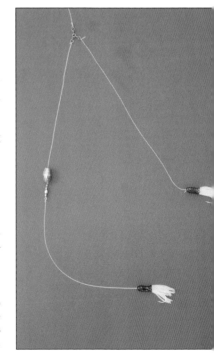

1-1/2 feet above the first. The rig is fairly simple to tie, but to save time replacing broken rigs on the water, Mullins and Lucius prepare several rigs before fishing, then wrap and secure them on thin wooden slats notched at each end. This allows the duo to keep extra rigs handy so little fishing time is wasted when a new rig is needed.

To make each rig, you need the following hardware components:

- One size 6 or 8 three-way swivel;
- One size 8 or 10 barrel swivel;
- One 1/4- to 1-oz. egg sinker (lighter for calm days or shallow bumping; heavier for windy days or deeper bumping);

The stump-bumper rig is simple to make and easy to use. Mullins and Lucius prepare multiple rigs before each fishing trip, keeping some handy as replacements in case of break-offs.

- Two 1/32- to 1/8-oz. jigheads (size also chosen to suit conditions);
- Two Southern Pro Lures Umbrella Crappie Tubes, Hot Grubs, Lit'l Hustlers or similar jig bodies; and
- 6- or 8-pound-test monofilament or fluorocarbon line.

"We like to use jigheads that have red hooks as opposed to bronze or gold," said Mullins. "These produce at least fifty percent more bites, which I believe is due to the fact that crappie see the red as blood on an injured baitfish and are quick to zero in on it. Jigheads with chartreuse hooks also work well at times, and we may change to those if the bite is slow."

"In fall, we'll typically spool our reels with eight- to ten-pound-test monofilament," Lucius said. "And the line used to make the rig itself will be a couple of pounds lighter. If you're using eight-pound main line, for example, the rig lines should be six-pound. In case of a hang-up, this allows the leader to be easily broken, then you're not wasting valuable time trying to get your lure unhung."

"I like to use camo monofilament on the leader lines," added Mullins. "This changes colors in the water, which helps it blend better, giving you one more advantage over the crappie. If you don't have camo, however, clear mono- or fluorocarbon line will work ok, too."

Making the Rig

Making the stump-bumper rig requires five basic steps:

Begin by tying an 18-inch mono- or fluorocarbon leader line to one eye of the three-way swivel.

Run this leader line through the egg sinker, then tie the tag end to the barrel swivel.

To the other eye of the barrel swivel, tie a 15-inch mono- or fluorocarbon leader to which one of the jigheads is tied.

Tie the other jighead to a 12-inch leader, and tie this leader to another eye of the three-way swivel. (The remaining three-way swivel eye ties to the main line from your reel.)

Rig the jig bodies on each jighead. The rig is then complete.

"We use a variety of Southern Pro jig bodies," said Mullins. "Typically, we prefer the Umbrella Crappie Tube, with its large flared skirt. But if we think it might help, we may change to another body type. The Hot Grubs, which have a curly tail on them, really drive crappie crazy in some situations where other lures aren't producing. And in muddy or deep water, the Glow Lit'l Hustlers, which are impregnated with luminescent, glow-in-the-dark material, may increase your catch rate. My

Mullins and Lucius carry a wide variety of jig body colors and styles they can use to determine the best crappie-fishing pattern on a given day.

favorite color is anything with chartreuse in it. But change colors or styles frequently until you determine the best pattern where you're fishing."

Lucius suggested carrying minnows on each trip as well as jigs. Sometimes, he said, it takes a marriage of live bait and artificial to produce the most crappie.

"Tipping a jighead/jig body combo with a live minnow may entice crappie to bite when the lure alone isn't working," he told me. "And, at times, it may be best to use only a jighead tipped with a minnow and dispense with the jig body altogether. Crappie can be real picky about they want, so once again, change up as often as necessary, or use different combinations on multiple poles until you determine what works best."

On-the-Water Action

The portion of Lake Conway we chose to fish was a big embayment the locals call "The Shale Pit." At first glance, it seems barren of cover, but in the 6- to 12-foot depths of the bay were numerous stumps scattered across the bottom, all clearly visible on the sonar unit handily mounted between the two bow seats of Mullins' boat.

"You can see crappie holding tight around these stumps," Lucius said, pointing to the fish icons on the unit's screen. "Or at least we hope they're crappie. What we'll do is get our poles ready and then motor up close to the stumps so the baits actually bump them. That's where the name stump bumping comes from."

The anglers had eight 12- to 16-foot B'n'M Capps & Coleman Series trolling rods paired with B'n'M's West Point spinning reels ready to go. These were placed in rod holders on Driftmaster T-Bars at the front of the boat, creating a big semicircle of poles on the craft's bow.

"These are great poles for this type of fishing," Mullins said. "But if it's windy and the water's rough, we may change over to B'n'M's Pro Staff trolling rods, which aren't as tip sensitive."

The stump-bumper rigs were deployed so the egg sinkers were dragging right on the bottom with the two jigs on each rig trailing behind. Then, with the two men in position, seated at the front of the boat, Mullins hit the foot-control on the bow-mounted trolling motor and maneuvered the boat back to a spot where we'd previously pinpointed numerous stumps and fish.

"You may have to do some scouting with your depthfinder first," he said, "then come back to the spots you've found and fish them. The idea is to approach the stumps very slowly and let the rigs bump right up against them. If you do this right, and crappie are there, you won't have to wait long for a bite."

As if on cue, one of the poles on Ricky's side of the boat went down, and he set the hook in a hefty crappie. One of Chris' poles took a nosedive about the same time, and he, too, lifted a nice crappie over the transom.

"It doesn't always work that quick," Ricky said. "But it's really a great technique, one that's easy to learn, that any angler can use to increase their catch of fall crappie."

We only had time to fish together for about an hour that day. During that time, however, we caught two dozen nice crappie.

I was doubly impressed with the efficiency of the stump-bumping technique when I asked other crappie anglers we saw if they were catching any fish. I talked with folks in six or eight other boats, and none had caught any crappie. The proprietor of the marina where we

Jeremy Mullins shows off a nice crappie caught while stump bumping with his father Chris on Grenada Lake, Mississippi. This specialized tactic produces fall slabs wherever it is used.

launched told me later that the bite was really off that day and almost no one was catching fish.

"There are lots of ways to catch fall crappie," Chris said as we were trailering the boat. "This is just one of them. But during our many years fishing for crappie, we've found that stump bumping is hard to beat when you're trying to catch fish this time of year. It's a tried-and-proven technique that'll put crappie in your livewell when nothing else works."

STUMP-BUMPING VARIATIONS

On the day I fished with Chris Mullins and Ricky Lucius, we found crappie holding primarily around stumps in 6 to 8 feet of water. The stump-bumping rig worked great in this situation, but can it be used in deeper or shallower water as well? Will it work on suspended fish?

"One of the nice things about the stump-bumping rig is the fact you can shorten the leader lines and use it even in very shallow waters," said Mullins. "And although you can put the sinker right on the bottom, you don't have to. When crappie are suspended in mid-depths, just present the rig at the level where you see fish on your fish finder and troll through the schools at a slow pace. The rig is very adaptable to a wide variety of situations."

To facilitate quick changeout of rigs made with different size hardware for different fishing conditions, Mullins and Lucius use a Kipper Enterprises No-Knot Fas-Snap, which ties to the main line and can be quickly clipped to one eye of the rig's three-way swivel.

FALL FISHING TIPS

A utumn is a golden season for crappie fishing fans. Summer's crowds have vanished. Lakes, ponds and rivers shimmer beneath canopies of vermilion and amber leaves. Summer-fattened crappie are in prime condition, offering exciting possibilities for action-hungry anglers.

This season offers some of the year's best crappie angling if you learn some tips that will help you find and tempt these silvery panfish. Read on, and you will.

Try Bluffs

Fall crappie often hold near steep vertical bluffs along the shoreline that allow quick movement from shallow to deep water and vice versa. This time of year, however, they may be anywhere between the bottom and the surface, making them difficult to pinpoint. Start by looking at the water clarity. If the water is discolored, light penetration will be restricted, and crappie will move shallower. Thus, the angler should begin by fishing shallow reaches first. If the water is clear, bright sunlight will drive most crappie into the depths or under heavy cover. In this situation, fish first around deeper hideouts. Efficiently check all depths until a crappie is caught, then work that depth thoroughly for additional fish.

Back out with the Fish

When fishing a reservoir that has current caused by power generation, it pays to observe changes in the amount of current. Crappie may be in as little as 4 to 5 feet of water when current is minimal, but when power generation increases and current is stronger, crappie will move out to structures 10 to 20 feet deep. In the latter situation, work offshore cover, positioning your boat directly above and dropping minnows straight down. Or back off and cast 1/8-ounce jigs dressed with tubes or curlytail grubs.

Get to the Point

If the water level starts dropping fast due to power generation, try fishing points using

The rocky bluff in the background produced this Lake Norfork slab for Arkansas angler Dena Woerner. Fall crappie frequent steep, vertical structures like this where they can move quickly from shallow water to deep and back again as water and weather conditions change.
PHOTO BY Noel Vick

Adding a scent product to your lure may increase hookups with sometimes fussy fall crappie.

small spinners. Retrieve the lure with an up-and-down motion, or buzz it along the surface and allow it to "die" and fall right beside the cover. Position your boat in deep water and cast toward the shallow part of the point, or vice versa.

Use Some Scents

When an autumn cold front passes, you may entice persnickety crappie to bite by adding liquid, gel or solid scent products to your lures. These often enhance the number of strikes you get when crappie are finicky. The fish will hold on longer, too, increasing your chance of getting good hooksets.

Fish Windward Shores

Wind can be an important factor in determining where you're most likely to find early-fall crappie. Wind pushes tiny invertebrates that minnows and other baitfish eat. If there's a westerly wind for a couple of days, an east-shore area could hold the most fish, or vice versa. Consequently, you should always give wind-hit areas your full attention.

Rock and Roll

During late fall, as aquatic vegetation dies, crappie often move to deep rock piles. The best are associated with humps, outside channel bends, saddles between rises and other prominent bottom structure. Fish them with a rig made by tying a 3/8- to 1/2-ounce bell sinker at your line's end. Place a snelled hook 12 inches above the sinker on a dropper loop, then tie a 1/16-ounce jig directly to your line 18 inches above the hook. Bait the hook with a lively minnow, then drag the rig across the bottom near the rock pile until you catch a crappie. When you find your quarry, position your boat right over the strike zone and switch to a vertical presentation, which will help you avoid spooking other crappie.

Cedars and Shad

Not all crappie hold on deep structures in late fall. Many follow schools of shad into the backs of feeder creeks, holding in 4 to 6 feet of water along the edges of channel breaks. If you can find cedar brush piles in such areas, chances are you've found a

Use a slip-bobber rig to work minnows over shallow cedar brush piles for hot fall action.

mother lode of crappie. Work them with a stationary slip-bobber-and-minnow rig, or use a vertical tightline tactic with jigs.

Try Bream-Like Lures

In ponds and small lakes, crappie often stay fat and healthy by eating a diet heavy on juvenile sunfish. In these waters, particularly those with clear water, your fall catch rate may soar if you fish with lures resembling tiny bream in color and/or shape. Jigs with some combination of red, gold and green colors work especially well in this situation, as do small sunfish-imitation crankbaits and spinners with gold blades and brightly colored bodies.

Return for Wayward Suspenders

At times, your fish finder may pinpoint a bit of key structure—an isolated stump, for example, or a rock pile—that is void of crappie. When you find such areas, slowly circle around that spot and look for suspended fish. If you find them, make note of the structure's location, then return to it later. You might find that these previously inactive crappie have moved onto the structure and begun feeding.

"See" Edges Out of Sight

Fall crappie often hold along creek-channel drop-offs and other edge areas. You can fish such a location better if you mark it with several buoys. Locate the drop-off with sonar, then slowly follow the edge. Throw out a marker buoy each time you cross a certain depth—10 feet, for instance. Continue placing the buoys, about 20 feet apart, until you've used them all. Now you have a visible image of the edge and can fish it more thoroughly for crappie.

Soft-Plastic Minnows

Although often overlooked by crappie anglers, realistic soft-plastic baitfish lures such as the Banjo Glitter Minnow and Snag Proof's Moss Master Swimmin' Shad are dynamite on fall crappie. They not only come in a variety of sizes and colors, but they're weedless as well, allowing you to place them right in the middle of thick cover, where crappie are likely to be.

PRO TIP

"When fishing in fall with jigs, give corks a try. When you locate the depth where crappie are holding, you can set the cork and therefore keep the jig in the strike zone. A cork also allows you to slow your presentation. Many times the fish will strike after you give the jig a small twitch and then let the jig stand still.

"When using a cork, always try to use one just big enough to hold up the size jig you are using. For this technique, many times a 1/48-ounce jighead is all you need, and this will allow you to use a very small cork. The fish will feel very little resistance."

—Russ Bailey, www.midwestcrappie.com

ICEBOX SLABS

The air was icy when we left the marina, but when we arrived at our fishing hole, the calm wind and warm sun made the morning feel pleasant despite the 25-degree temperature.

It was January 23. I was fishing on west Arkansas' Lake Greeson, one of the country's top big-crappie destinations, with my oldest son Josh and friends Alex Hinson and Lewis Peeler. Fishing guide Jerry Blake of Action Fishing Trips had promised to put us on some nice cold-weather slabs, and, bundled up like Eskimos, we were waiting on him to fulfill that pledge. We didn't have to wait long.

"One on red!" Jerry snapped.

Each of us was watching "color-coded" slip bobbers above our minnow baits, and Alex's red float had sunk slowly out of sight. A light-biting winter crappie had inhaled the minnow on that line.

"Dadgummit!" Alex exclaimed as he grabbed the pole and snapped it upward without hooking a fish.

"One on green!" Jerry said. "And one on black!"

Alex's red float was back under, too, and Jerry had a hit on the jig he was fishing at the front of the boat.

Suddenly, everyone had a fish on, and with a bit of maneuvering, we managed to land four of the five.

"They feel like ice," Lewis said as he felt the sides of the crappie he caught. "I don't know how they can be so lively and be so cold."

Catching slow-biting winter crappie can be tough at times, but anglers who know tips for success probably will learn that cold-water fishing isn't as difficult as they imagined.

Lively they were, though. Most fish we caught that day barely wiggled the bobber when they took the bait, but each fought hard when hooked. We hooked plenty, too, a fact that made this polar adventure highly enjoyable.

Catching winter crappie can be challenging. Cold-water crappie may bite so gingerly they are almost undetectable. Add to that the fact that winter crappie stay near deep cover and structure where they often are difficult to find, and it's little wonder many anglers who try for crappie this season give up in frustration.

Despite the aggravations, however, crappie fishing when it's cold offers special rewards. For one thing, cold-weather crappie often gather in large, compact schools, so where you catch one fish, chances are excellent you'll catch several more. It's not unusual to find a dozen or more on a single piece of cover.

Bigger fish seem to be the norm this season as well. Young-of-the-year crappie have grown, and adult fish have added weight after months feasting on abundant shad, minnows and other forage. The average size is larger as a result. And when a big crappie is caught, chances are good the ones with it will be sizeable as well.

In addition, these cold crappie are superb on the dinner table. Coming straight from nature's icebox keeps them fresh and tasty.

Winter Basics

In winter, more than any season, crappie are deep-water fish. Deep is a relative thing, however, and you need to know some characteristics of the lake you're fishing to

Finding the right type of superstructure allowed the author (left) and his friend Alex Hinson to catch this big mess of winter crappie on Arkansas' DeGray Lake.   PHOTO BY Jerry Blake

enjoy success. When fishing a shallow, heavily timbered impoundment with average depths in the 10- to 20-foot range, for example, you may find crappie holding no more than 8 to 15 feet deep. In a large, open reservoir on the other hand, especially one in the mountains, water may reach 100 feet deep or more, and crappie may spend the winter at depths of 25 to 40 feet, sometimes more. Many of these fish will be suspended, avoiding deeper water where less oxygen, forage and cover make conditions uncomfortable for living.

Water clarity also may influence crappie depth. In muddy waters, fish tend to stay somewhat shallower. In clear water, they go deeper.

When the water is cold, features holding crappie are more likely to be offshore, often in mid-lake. These include creek/river channels, humps, inundated ponds, man-made fish attractors, timbered bars, the deep ends of points and such. It's important to remember, however, crappie won't be evenly dispersed around these features. Instead, they'll be attracted to smaller, specific components of the larger structures called "superstructure." Finding these requires the aid of a good sonar unit.

Let's say, for example, you've found a creek channel meandering across the bottom of the lake—not a difficult thing to do. Crappie won't be along the entire length of the channel, however. Instead, they'll gather in compact schools where the channel exhibits a change of some sort. This may be a bit of cover where a secondary channel intersects the main channel, or around a tall tree standing on a sharp bend in the channel—anything different from the norm. Finding these types of super-structure with a good fish finder can mean the difference between catching lots of winter crappie or none at all.

Building and Fishing Crappie Attractors

One way to narrow the scope of your search is placing your own fish attractors in areas likely to be used by winter crappie. Jerry Blake has done this in Arkansas' Lake Greeson, a reservoir completed in 1950 where most natural cover has long since rotted away. His "crappie condos" are made from 20-foot-long bundles of giant cane (bamboo) run through and weighted with cinder blocks so they lay horizontally on the bottom or placed upright in 5-gallon buckets of concrete. The condos he and his clients fish in winter are sunk near deep channels, inside creek-channel bends and drop-offs from flats to creek channels, all prime hotspots this season. He records the depth of each condo in a notebook, marks it as a waypoint on his GPS, then writes down the coordinates. He then can return to each of the hundreds of crappie condos he's created and fish those appropriate for the season.

When our group fished with Blake in January, the depth at which the crappie were holding varied from one condo to another. On some, Blake's fish finder showed

Arkansas crappie guide Jerry Blake (right) helped client Jim Erickson catch these nice winter crappie on a bamboo fish attractor in Arkansas' Lake Greeson. Blake sinks these attractors in key locations throughout the year, then fishes around those in deeper water to catch cold-weather slabs.

crappie 18 feet deep; on others, they were 23 feet down. But the fishing rig this guide uses makes adjustments easy.

A Thill 1/2-inch, pencil-style slip bobber is rigged beneath a bobber stop and plastic bead and above a No. 6 Eagle Claw Aberdeen hook. Two split shot are added between hook and float (one near the hook and one about 4 inches above the hook), and the hook is baited with a live minnow. Blake uses 10-foot jig poles, like B'n'M's Richard Williams Crappie Wizard Series, which keep the rigs away from the boat so his clients aren't directly above the cover they're fishing. Several rigged poles are placed in rod holders along one side of the boat, the bobber stops are positioned at the depth where crappie are seen on the fish finder, then using a trolling motor, Blake slowly circles each fish attractor. Crappie often pull several floats down simultaneously, a testament to this tactic's effectiveness. If sonar reveals fish at a different depth as the boat moves from one condo to another, the bobber stop can easily be moved up or down to adjust the depth at which the bait suspends beneath the float.

"Hovering" for Deep Crappie

Crappie-fishing partners Kent Driscoll of Cordova, Tennessee, and John Harrison of Calhoun City, Mississippi, both members of the B'n'M Poles Pro Staff, also employ a multi-pole, slip-bobber set-up when fishing for deep-freeze crappie. The multitude of lakes they fish this season frequently lack man-made cover, however, so they often must sweep the water over deep natural structure such as creek channels and ledges to find schools of winter crappie.

"You often must crawl like a terrapin to catch wintertime crappie," says Driscoll. "Crappie this season are sluggish and won't go far to eat. When they do bite, it's usually a very subtle strike versus an aggressive one. Spider trolling with Thill corks helps us catch them."

They call their method "hovering."

"Corks allow you to move super slow, to 'hover' over structure," Driscoll says. "Crappie do not feel any resistance as they might when you're tightlining. Typically, a crappie will bite and then spit the bait. But because they don't feel resistance with a cork, they hold the bait longer, giving an angler a better chance of catching the fish."

I fished with Driscoll and Harrison on a freezing February day on Mississippi's Lake Washington. They placed six 10- to

Pro anglers John Harrison (left) and Kent Driscoll use "hovering"—fishing minnows or jigs under slip bobbers—to catch winter crappie over deep natural structure.

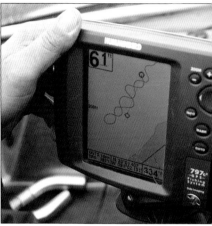

Mississippi anglers Don Terry (left) and Bernard Williams pioneered a multi-pole, slow-trolling tactic called "wildcatting" that draws reaction strikes from winter crappie. The screen of their fish finder shows the twisting path their boat followed on one wildcatting run.

12-foot B'n'M poles, each rigged with a live minnow or jig, in T-bars at the front of their boat. The Thill Premium Balsa Floats they use have the amount of weight the cork will float printed right on the brightly colored bobber, allowing them to select the proper size for detecting even the lightest bites.

The tactic worked. The duo caught several 2-pound-plus slabs during our morning of fishing.

"Wildcat Trolling" for Offshore Slabs

Bernard Williams and Don Terry of Jackson, Mississippi, are members of the Magnolia Crappie Club. When these experts seek winter crappie, they often fish along offshore bottom channels using a highly effective, multi-pole long-lining tactic they've dubbed "wildcat trolling."

"Wildcatting works great on cold-weather crappie," says Williams. "The method involves making constant turns while slow-trolling with multiple poles over river and creek ledges. Rods should be placed on the far left and far right sides of the boat. Boat speed should be around 0.4 to 0.5 mph. Sometimes I even stop completely and then take off."

Williams and Terry demonstrated the tactic for me one winter day, using their GPS unit to first locate a distinctive bottom channel, then zigzagging back and forth over the channel as they followed it in their boat. When they showed me the track marked on their GPS during this maneuvering, it looked like a series of interconnected loops.

"The turns allow the outside baits to come up while the inside baits fall, causing a reaction bite from either side," Williams says. "Each turn should be a long S turn. Then turn around and let the S overlap, creating a figure-eight. This method allows you to completely cover both sides of the ledge. Because crappie are predators, they attack when they see this bait speed up and slow down."

These fishing partners typically use tandem-rigged jigs or Blakemore Road Runners when wildcatting. On this day, the up-down motion of Road Runners proved irresistible to several hefty slabs.

Simple Works, Too

While the rigs discussed so far are hard to beat for winter crappie, you don't always need complicated configurations of terminal tackle to catch fish. Simple works, too.

Try tying on a small spoon and jigging it in deep water around standing snags. Use a slow, steady retrieve to work a spinner across a hump or point. Lower a jig to a school of crappie you've found with your fish finder and let it sit motionless until a fish can't resist it anymore. Uncomplicated methods such as these often catch as many cold-water crappie as more complex strategies, and you can spend more time relaxing and enjoying yourself when your favorite lake is likely to be pleasantly uncrowded.

Winter fishing isn't for everybody. Some prefer a warm fireplace inside to a frigid outing on a cold lake. If the fishing itch gets too intense to bear, though, give winter crappie a try. Fishing for these sassy panfish is a sure remedy for what ails you.

PIER PRESSURE

Most winter crappie anglers fish from boats because, during this season, most crappie move to offshore cover. Fishing from shore can be difficult when your quarry is out of reach.

If inclement weather keeps you shorebound this season, however, try fishing at the end of a public fishing pier. When such a structure is built, a deeper hole usually is created near the outside end, and frequently, brush piles are added to attract crappie. When the weather is cold outside, the fishing can be excellent.

In late December, on an Arkansas lake, I watched a pair of pier fishermen catch their thirty-fish limits of crappie in two hours by fishing such a place. These fellows were fishing live minnows under slip bobbers, but I caught a few slabs myself casting a Blakemore Road Runner to edges of cover at the end of the pier. A slow, steady retrieve proved irresistible to fifteen hefty crappie, including a 17-incher that weighed more than 2 pounds.

PRO TIP

"I like to target deep-water piers in winter. I downsize everything—line, weight, hook and, most importantly, the bait—when doing this. I like to tip a 1/32-ounce jig with a small minnow, then add scent to the jig so crappie hold the bait longer, resulting in better hook sets. I use Berkley Crappie Nibbles and inject them into the jig skirt with a Bait Pump. I fish this combo on a 12-foot B'n'M ultralight pole, targeting the crossbars under each pier. When the bite is tough, I go to a cork-and-minnow rig fished the same way."

—Hugh Krutz, www.thebaitpump.com

PRO TIP

"Winter is my favorite time to target crappie. During this season, crappie bunch up in large schools and suspend over deep water and creek ledges. White crappie tend to gang up in creeks, and black crappie bunch up in deep water targeting threadfin shad. Crappie will be around big schools of shad, so if your electronics are showing large schools of shad, you know crappie are right below ready to ambush the baitfish. Anglers can rig up with live bait or jigs. Crappie will hit both in deep water in winter."

—Wally Marshall, www.mrcrappie.com

CHRISTMAS-TREE CRAPPIE

Winter crappie usually hold on deep cover and structure, making them somewhat difficult to locate. In recent years, though, fisheries managers have sought to bring crappie and anglers together by placing man-made fish attractors in many first-rate crappie lakes.

These artificial crappie "condos" usually are made from trees bundled together with wire and sunk with concrete weights. They're especially helpful to anglers unfamiliar with a lake's bottom topography and to those who don't have sophisticated electronic equipment for locating crappie concentrations on underwater structure. Fish attractors placed by government agencies usually are marked with special buoys or signs, so all an angler must do to find crappie is find the markers and then move from one fish-attractor to another, working jigs and minnows through the woody tangles below.

How Man-Made Fish Attractors Work

Fishermen have been sinking brush and trees to attract and concentrate fish for hundreds of years. Sink a tree in a lake where much of the natural cover has disappeared, and crappie will flock to it like a new restaurant in town. These sites give crappie a place to rest and feed and also provide potential spawning habitat.

Old Christmas trees are among the most often used materials for making crappie attractors. These usually are gathered at advertised collection sites, tied in bundles and anchored with concrete blocks to supplement existing cover. Within a few days after the trees are sunk, small aquatic organisms gather around the maze of branches and twigs. When baitfish discover these minute food

Fishing underwater fish attractors made from old Christmas trees and other materials is a surefire way to zero in on schools of winter crappie.

Stake beds made from wooden slats driven into a lake bed are excellent fish attractors where crappie can be caught year-round.

animals, they begin schooling around the brush piles to feed on the invertebrates. Crappie soon follow, feeding on the schools of baitfish. Then fishermen can zero in on the concentrations of crappie.

Christmas trees aren't the only material used for building crappie attractors. As mentioned in the previous chapter, some anglers like Jerry Blake use cane or bamboo as the primary material. Another variation uses several small hardwood trees bundled together with wire. Wooden stake beds also work well. Long, thin slats of lumber are driven into the lake bed or nailed to shipping pallets for sinking in deeper water. Many state agencies use bundles of old tires with holes punched in them to facilitate sinking. Concrete blocks attached with wire hold the attractors on the bottom.

The Barkley Lake Brush Pile Study

A study on Lake Barkley, a 57,920-acre reservoir in Kentucky and Tennessee, proved that Christmas-tree fish shelters attract more and larger crappie than areas without such structures. The study showed that each acre of brush averaged 1,530 crappie, while an acre without brush contained only 319 crappie. In areas with brush, crappie were ten times larger in average weight than areas without brush piles.

Based on this data, the Kentucky Department of Fish and Wildlife Resources, the Tennessee Wildlife Resources Agency and the Tennessee Valley Authority began placing brush-pile fish attractors in several Tennessee Valley reservoirs, including Barkley and Kentucky lakes. Tens of thousands of individual structures were placed in dozens of lakes.

Over the years since they were first placed in these lakes, fish attractors have helped heighten Kentucky and Barkley lakes' reputations as two of the country's finest crappie fisheries. Using maps available to help pinpoint brush piles, even first-time visitors can cash in on the bonanza of blue-ribbon crappie fishing served up by these enormous impoundments.

The Bull Shoals/Norfork Fish Cover Project

Another large-scale fish attractor project took place in lakes Bull Shoals and Norfork, two large U.S. Army Corps of Engineers impoundments on the Arkansas-Missouri state line.

The Corps completed construction of Norfork Lake in 1944 and Bull Shoals Lake in 1952. The main purpose of these reservoirs was to provide flood control and hydropower. During construction, virtually all trees were removed from what would later be the lakes' bottoms. The trees that were not removed have mostly rotted away, and only trunks remain.

Because the lake levels fluctuate dramatically, aquatic vegetation has never become well established in Norfork and Bull Shoals. Lack of cover has always limited fish production. Still, crappie and other fish grow very fast in the clear, high-quality water, and fishing is excellent for those who know where to find their quarry. Unfortunately, lack of cover made it difficult for many anglers to locate concentrations of sportfish.

In 1986, the Twin Lakes Chapter of the Bass Research Foundation approached the Arkansas Game and Fish Commission with a special request. They wanted assistance introducing aquatic vegetation into Norfork and Bull Shoals to improve fish habitat and fishing. At the time, the Corps and the Commission were concerned that establishing aquatic vegetation might conflict with other reservoir uses. The Game and Fish Commission suggested that a large-scale artificial habitat improvement project might accomplish some of the same goals.

A plan involving use of trees from the lakes' shorelines to create fish attractors was presented to the Corps and the U.S. Fish Wildlife Service for federal funding approval through the Sportfish Restoration Act. Both federal agencies and the Twin

Fishing sunken brush piles is easier if you first delineate the boundaries of each fish attractor using marker buoys.

Lakes Chapter of Bass Research Foundation approved the plan, and the project began in earnest in 1987.

Since the project began, more than 600 fish attractors have been installed in Bull Shoals and Norfork. More than 70,000 trees comprise the attractors, which cover over 160 acres of lake bottom totaling 33 miles in length.

Each attractor is composed of thirty or more bundles of trees (six or less trees per bundle, depending on size) and covers an area approximately 40 feet wide and 300 feet long. The bundles were sunk along a contour line that corresponds to the depth at which the thermocline usually forms (25 feet deep). On Bull Shoals, the target elevation is 630 feet above mean sea level (msl), and on Norfork, it's 525 feet above msl. Fishermen can figure out how deep the attractors are by calling a Corps lake information line, getting the current lake levels and subtracting the above elevations.

Fish attractors have been placed in many other Arkansas lakes as well. These include outstanding crappie waters such as Bob Kidd, Elmdale, Chicot, Dierks, DeQueen, Sugarloaf, Hinkle and several lakes on Dagmar Wildlife Management Area.

In other states, fish attractors now are common features in many first-rate crappie lakes as well. All such lakes offer excellent winter crappie angling for those who know how to fish sunken brush piles.

Fishing Brush Piles

Bill Fletcher of Mountain Home, Arkansas, has guided fishermen on Lake Norfork for more than thirty years. He's done an extensive fish-attractor program on his own

Anglers young and old can quickly learn successful methods for catching crappie on man-made fish attractors.

for his guide service and was instrumental in the completion of the Lake Norfork fish-cover project.

"Lake Norfork was over ninety percent cleared when it was built," he says. "Now the brush piles placed in the lake are magnets for crappie and other species like bass and wall-eyes.

"These brush piles can make a big difference for crappie fishermen," Fletcher continues, "especially someone fishing a big deep lake like Norfork for the first time. One of the biggest helps for me as a guide is, I can take someone out who's never fished here before, and on a half-a-day trip, I can show them how to locate brush piles with a graph and how to fish them. Then they can come back to the lake and have a successful fishing trip on their own."

After choosing a fish attractor site marked with a buoy, Fletcher runs his boat over the site, using a graph recorder to determine the positioning of the brush.

"On Norfork and Bull Shoals, the brush piles will extend about 100 to 150 feet on each side of the buoy, and about ninety percent of them will be centered on the twenty- to twenty-five-foot depth," Fletcher notes. "Begin by using your graph to find the shallowest brush pile, and mark it with a buoy. Crappie in an aggressive or 'biting' posture often will be lined up horizontally above the shallowest brush piles, so fish these piles first."

Fletcher recommends a count-down technique for pinpointing feeding fish.

"Take your boat a cast away from your marker buoy, twenty or thirty feet, and using four-pound-test line and a

Bait and tackle shops often carry lake maps that show the locations of permanent brush piles and other fish attractors.

1/16-ounce jig head, cast to the buoy," he says. "Now count the jig down until you get a hit or hit brush. If you get a hit, use the same count next cast. If you hit brush, use a shorter count.

"The key to catching crappie on fish attractors is positive depth control," Fletcher continues. "Crappie don't feed down; they bite up. So don't fish under them. Sometimes crappie will form horizontal schools on the sides of the brush piles, but the same tactics will work if you can locate them.

"You can catch crappie without the brush piles," says Fletcher, "but brush piles certainly make it easier. You establish the fish are there and at a certain depth, then boom, boom, boom, you're putting them in the boat."

Now the old excuse, "Winter crappie are too hard to find," just doesn't hold water. With a map and sonar, any crappie angler can easily find man-made fish attractors holding plenty of big slabs. Where fish shelters are marked with buoys, it's even easier.

Don't wait for the spring spawn to enjoy the thrill of crappie fishing. Bundle up and indulge in some first-rate fishing fun. Christmas-tree crappie provide a sure cure for winter's cabin blues.

RECYCLE CHRISTMAS TREES

You can build your own crappie attractors by recycling Christmas trees after the holiday season. Attach a concrete block to the base of each tree to anchor it. If placed in deep enough water, the trees will stand upright, and due to the upward sweep of the branches, your hook won't be easily snagged when you work jigs or minnows around them.

For most anglers, a few properly placed fish attractors are adequate. Place some deep, some shallow, some on flats, some on ledges and stream channels, and you'll always have a productive crappie spot regardless of the time of year. Plot the locations of the attractors on a GPS to guide you to the exact spot. When you are in the immediate area of the cover, you can spot it with sonar or fan-cast jigs to locate it.

Some government agencies such as the U.S. Army Corps of Engineers have restrictions on placing crappie cover in their lakes. Check for such restrictions before placing your cover in any public water.

TIPS FOR FISHING CRAPPIE ATTRACTORS

- Ease your anchor to the bottom on either side of the attractor to avoid spooking crappie. Or use a trolling motor to slowly fish around the attractor.
- Lower your bait or lure until you feel the brush, then take note of that depth so you are constantly working within the crappie's strike zone. Fish minnows stationary below a bobber set at the proper depth. Move jigs or small spoons slowly up and down in and around the brush.
- Crankbaits, spinners and jig/spinner combos can be cast from a boat anchored to one side of an attractor. Work the lure over the brush pile's top or along the sides.
- Thin wire hooks bend easily, lessening the need for re-rigging due to hang-ups.

PRO TIP

"If you set your own crappie structure in a lake, consider using five-gallon plastic buckets to make artificial stumps. Fill them about three-fourths full of gravel and set them in the lake. The plastic will never rot. Within a month, the fish can't tell the difference between a bucket or a stump. I usually throw a marker out and put ten to twelve buckets around the marker. I have done this in several places on Kentucky Lake and made stump fields. The buckets are cheap, they're easy to put out and they work."

—Richard Williams,
Kentucky Lake crappie guide

WINTER FISHING TIPS

Fishing for winter crappie can be beautifully simple. Yet many crappie anglers take this simplicity a step too far. One or two proven tactics and baits command most of their fishing time, and if these don't produce . . . well, there's always next time.

You can greatly improve your winter crappie-fishing success by trying a few new concepts and techniques. Stick to traditional approaches when they're producing slabs. But when "regular" tactics don't work, the following tricks can make your catch rate soar.

Draglining

Draglining—trolling with a bottom-weighted crappie rig—is an excellent method for pinpointing hard-to-find winter slabs in deep water along creek channels, humps and other bottom structure. Attach a 1-ounce bank sinker to the end of your main line. Above this are two to four 12-inch-long drop lines spaced about 18 inches apart. Each drop line is connected to the main line via a loop knot or three-way swivel. Jigs, minnows, jig/minnow combos or a combination of these are tied to the drops.

While wind drifting or slow trolling with an electric motor, work the rig vertically beside the boat using a "lift, drop" action. When you feel the rig bump against cover or structure, raise it up and over. The angler must be attentive at all times, raising or lowering the rig with the rod tip to maintain "feel" with the rig below and keep

The winter crappie angler can use many proven tactics to catch nice crappie like this in cold water.

it bouncing across the pieces of cover and structure without hanging. Strikes often come just as the rig is lowered behind woody cover.

Winter Springs

Underwater springs bubbling up in the bottom of a lake often attract concentrations of winter crappie. Spring water stays at a constant temperature year-round, usually between 60 and 70 degrees, thus providing a place where crappie warm up in winter. Temperature gauges can help locate springs, or use an outdoor thermometer tied to a string to detect changes in water temperature. Watch, too, for springs that reveal their presence by altering the surface of the water slightly. The water around a spring is usually clearer than the rest of a lake, so use lighter line and smaller, realistic lures or live minnows.

Try a Combo

The jig/minnow combination—a marriage of crappie fishing's two most popular enticements—is perhaps the best of all winter crappie-catchers. The two together often nab crappie when either alone won't work, so carry jigs *and* minnows on all your cold-weather fishing trips.

Trap Your Quarry

Vertical jigging with a small lipless crankbait such as the Bill Lewis Tiny Trap or Cotton Cordell's C21 Super Spot is deadly on winter crappie suspended around structure such as sunken islands, rock ridges and logs. Position your boat over the target structure, then lower the lure to the bottom. Engage your reel and take up slack. Jerk the lure off the bottom 2 to 3 feet, and let it free-fall. Maneuver your boat along structure, jigging the lure this way.

Get Small

Cold-water crappie sometimes ignore the 1/16- and 1/32-ounce jigs many anglers use. This season you may do better by dropping to a smaller size— 1/100 ounce, 1/64 ounce or 1/48. Tinier jigs drop slower, more naturally, in the water. That can make an important difference in your catch rate when fish aren't aggressive.

It's hard to beat a jig/minnow combo for winter crappie catching.

Farm Fishing

Farm ponds provide possibilities for shore anglers. First, be sure the pond contains crappie; many don't. If it does, and the owner grants permission to fish, you're in business. Head to the levee that impounds the water. Big slabs frequently are taken by casting to woody cover here. My favorite lure in this situation is a large safety-pin spinner, but carry of a variety of lures, and keep changing until you determine what is most productive.

Look for Ledges

When using sonar, scan for shallow underwater ledges—ditches, cuts and gullies—near bankside bluffs or coves. Ledges are especially productive when found near timber, brush piles or other crappie cover.

One-sixteenth to 1/8-ounce jigs are ideal lures for fishing ledges. Work a jig down the drop-off, hopping it in stairstep fashion until you get a hit.

Use a GPS

GPS units are more affordable than ever, with some handheld units priced less than $100. These high-tech marvels translate satellite signals into data an angler can use to return to first-rate winter fishing areas such as brush piles and open-water drop-offs. Don't waste time triangulating with landmarks or watching a fish finder to find your favorite winter fishing holes. Learn to use a GPS and you can be fishing instead of looking.

Seek Power

Many crappie lakes provide cooling water for adjacent nuclear and coal-fired power plants. Such waters provide some of the fastest winter action available. Shad are attracted to warm-water releases from the plant, and crappie follow to gorge on the bounty. Look for thick black bands on your fish finder that indicate baitfish schools, then fish at the same depth using shad-like crankbaits, spinners, bladebaits or tandem-rigged jigs. Big catches of slab crappie often result.

Warm discharges from lakeside power plants attract crappie looking for an easy meal of shad.

Head for the Headwaters

Headwater areas tend to produce the best winter fishing. These are the upper ends of lakes, usually opposite the dam, where the major stream or streams feeding the lake flow into it. Late-winter crappie become active earlier in headwaters because this is where the water first begins to warm. Creeks and small streams above the lake warm first because they are shallow and fed by the first warming rains. These in turn feed larger streams flowing into the lake, and they, too, warm up before the deeper main lake.

Remember this when planning a fishing trip this time of year. Headwaters usually outproduce other portions of a lake.

Whistler Jigs

Northland Tackle's Whistler Jig has a uniquely designed spinner blade that helps provoke strikes from lethargic winter crappie. It's especially effective in dingy water situations. Secure a live minnow to the bait-holding collar on the hook shank and free-spool the combo to brush piles and stumps with a vertical presentation. As the Whistler Jig helicopters down, it falls slowly and enticingly, at half the speed of equally weighted jigs. Crappie find it hard to resist.

Add a minnow to a Whistler Jig and let it helicopter down through the water to coax a hit from sluggish winter crappie.

Soft Strikes

When a winter crappie strikes, it usually feels "soft," like the bait has picked up a leaf or little stick. Be prepared to set the hook the instant your line goes slack or your bait doesn't feel right. Learn to be a line watcher. Using fluorescent line and wearing polarized sunglasses improves your ability to detect subtle strikes.

PRO TIP

"I like to fish concrete pilings on docks, bridges and other structures in winter. Concrete heats up during the day and then holds heat. This causes the water around the pilings to be slightly warmer than other water. Baitfish are attracted to the algae and warm water, and they, in turn, attract crappie. I use small jigs like the Southern Pro Stinger to fish the cross-members and then down to the pad each piling sits on. Start shallow and move deeper as the day progresses."

—Bernard Williams,
Magnolia Crappie Club, Mississippi

TACTICAL TIPS

SPIDER TROLLING
FOR CRAPPIE

S pider trolling, or spider rigging, as it often is called, is a tactic that should be part of every crappie angler's arsenal. The name originates from the use of multiple poles jutting from the front, back and/or sides of the boat, which gives the craft the appearance of a colossal spider with legs pointing in all directions. Few methods are better suited for finding often-scattered schools of crappie.

Spider trolling may involve the use of as few as two poles or as many as sixteen, but six to eight are most commonly used. The poles—long, graphite or graphite-composite trolling or jigging poles, or sometimes cane poles—are held in rod holders. Some anglers still use C-clamp rod holders that can be screwed down tight on the boat's gunwales wherever the angler wants them. Better, though, are high-quality "T-bar" holders like those made by Driftmaster that won't slip off or twist to the side like the old C-clamps. These have two to eight rod holders attached to a crossbar, and each crossbar is on an upright that has a bottom bracket for securing the T-bar in the boat. When properly placed, these T-bar holders allow the angler to fish with several poles spread out at regular intervals across the front, back and/or sides of the boat, a few inches to a foot or two apart. Rigged this way, the angler can drift with the wind or troll with an electric motor and sweep a broad area of water with a variety of baits to find crappie.

Why do they call it spider trolling? When you see it done, with all the poles sticking out like spider legs, the reason is obvious.

Many of today's crappie anglers use special-made T-bar rod holders for arranging their poles when spider trolling. A fish finder nearby allows the angler to stay near crappie-holding structure and cover when trolling.

The number of poles used when spider trolling depends to a large extent on the ability of the angler. The fewer the number of poles, the simpler the fishing. As the number of poles increases, it becomes more difficult to keep lines and baits from tangling and to hook and land fish, especially when there are multiple bites. As with so many things, practice makes perfect.

Determine beforehand if there are any restrictions on the body of water you'll be fishing. On some lakes, you can fish with as many poles as you like; elsewhere, the number is limited.

Spider Trolling Basics

Most spider riggers start by using a variety of baits or lures rigged at different depths. For example, when using six poles, four might be rigged with jigs in different colors and sizes, and the other two with minnows. Two baits might be set 6 feet deep, two at 8, and two at 10. This allows testing different baits and depths until you find actively feeding crappie. When you determine crappie favor a certain depth or bait, then all the poles are rigged to conform to that preference.

Almost any bait or lure that entices crappie can be used. Jigs and live minnows are the choice of most anglers, but crankbaits, spinners, spoons and other crappie-catchers may be used as well.

Anglers with big boats sometimes mount one or two pedestal seats on the front deck just behind the T-bar rod holders. This allows the angler to sit comfortably within reach of the poles while fishing. A sonar fish finder also can be mounted here to aid in following bottom channels and other crappie-attracting structure while trolling.

Some anglers prefer to push their rigs, with all poles at the front of the boat. Some prefer to pull them, with all the rigs at the stern. Some do both at once and may include poles along the boat's sides as well. All these variations work well. The one you use will depend to a large extent on how proficient you become at spider trolling and how many anglers your boat will accommodate. When rigs are spread around the front, sides and back, you'll need a fishermen near each spread to land hooked crappie. A single angler in a small johnboat may be able to accomplish this with no trouble. In bigger crafts where several anglers are fishing, you may prefer having poles at all points of the compass.

If the wind is blowing, you can get by without a trolling motor, but you're not likely to catch as many crappie. Wind drifting is a one-way, time-consuming affair: make a drift, take up the lines, motor back up, reset the lines, drift again. A trolling motor allows constant fishing without fuss. It also permits you to vary your speed and control direction, important factors when chasing fussy crappie.

The Right Rig

There are many different rigs you can use on your spider-rig poles. One of the simplest is made by attaching a 1-ounce bank sinker to the end of your main line. Above this are two to four 12- to 18-inch-long drop lines (shorter lines on top, longer on bottom) spaced about 18 inches apart. Each drop line is connected to the main line via a loop knot or swivel. Jigs or 1 to 2/0 Aberdeen crappie hooks are tied to the drop lines. If hooks are used, they are baited with live minnows. If you like, you can tip jigs with minnows as well, for extra enticement. The finished rigs are lowered to the bottom, then you just start trolling.

Speed

Speed probably is the most important aspect of spider trolling, but there's no magic formula for determining what speed is best under a given set of conditions. On some days you may have to inch your boat along to get strikes. On other days you must troll much faster to

This angler has an ideal set-up for trolling: holders for several poles, an electric motor to help maintain the proper speed and a fish finder in front of him that can be watched to enable trolling over good cover and structure. The result: crappie on the hook.

catch fish. And when you find the productive speed, you must maintain it, even when wind or current push your boat ahead or drive it back.

A good starting point is about 1.5 to 2 mph, but savvy anglers experiment with different trolling speeds until they determine what is most effective. This varies with the type of bait used and the measure of water clarity. For example, you might troll minnows or small spinners very slowly for crappie in a lake muddied by heavy rain. Crappie feed primarily by sight. In discolored water they may have a difficult time pinpointing a tiny, fast-moving jig but have little trouble homing in on a shiner or flashy spinnerbait slowly passing by.

In a clear-water lake, jigs may be very effective even at faster trolling speeds. Then again, they may not produce at all. The key word here is *experiment*. Try to figure how crappie are likely to react in the type water you're fishing, then adapt your tactics to conform to those expectations. But if your game plan doesn't produce within a short time, try something different. Sooner or later, the innovative crappie angler discovers a pattern for capitalizing on the situation.

One mistake crappie anglers often make is trolling at the same boat speed when headed into the wind as when headed with the wind. On an otherwise still lake, you travel faster with the wind than against it, assuming you never reposition your electric motor throttle. Therefore, in order to maintain your ideal trolling speed, you must adjust the throttle up or down depending on which way you are traveling.

These factors may explain why you catch crappie when trolling in one direction and not in the other.

Off and Running

Some anglers start their troll blind; they have no idea what type of structure or cover is beneath the water. They simply start trolling and hope their hit-and-miss tactics produce more hits than misses.

Spider trolling is one of the best tactics for finding often-scattered schools of crappie, particularly when fishing unfamiliar lakes.

It's best, however, to use sonar to pinpoint structure and cover crappie favor—woody cover along the edges of creek and river channels, long points, rock piles rising into lighted water, man-made fish attractors, etc.—and troll over that. With a serious look at a bottom contour map and a quick check of prominent bottom changes with sonar, you could be catching slabs in minutes instead of wandering aimlessly.

Try zigzagging over channel breaks and adjacent flats. Stump fields and weed edges at proper depths may be good early and late when crappie are more likely to be feeding. In summer, crappie are likely to be strung out along the thermocline in a shallow plane, so covering large areas of water by trolling may enable you to catch more of these fish within a given range.

When you find schooling crappie, throw out a marker buoy so you can anchor just outside the school and cast to it, or continue to troll around the concentration. A savvy angler may take crappie from one of these marked spots for an hour or more if the fish aren't spooked.

Crappie aren't hard to catch, but at times they're hard to find. Spider trolling, done properly, can help you overcome that problem. Practice this method and you'll rarely need to stop by the fish market on the way home.

SPIDER TROLLING TIPS

- How much line should you have out when trolling? When fishing jigs or minnows, most crappie anglers let out 50 to 75 feet. On windy days, they fish even farther back. The ideal distance varies with water clarity, speed, bait type and other factors. Experiment to see what works best.

A long-handled net assures you'll land more "papermouths" when using the long poles typical of spider trolling.

- The number of lines that can be trolled effectively depends to some degree on the experience of the angler. Experts sometimes can handle up to sixteen, but most beginners should start with no more than two.
- Let the motion of the boat do the hooksetting. Wait until the pole has a definite bend in it, then remove it from the holder and boat the fish. Don't stop the trolling motor. Before you get the first fish off, another may be on.

PRO TIP

"When spider trolling in spring, most people will stay in water 10 feet or deeper. They are afraid the trolling motor will scare the fish if they get shallow. Don't be afraid to get into 1 to 2 feet of water. I catch a lot of fish in very shallow water.

"Also, when spider trolling in very shallow water, keep the drags set very loose. When fishing real shallow, the fish will grab the bait and take off fast. If the drag is not set loose, the hook will rip out of their mouth. Let the fish run out enough line so you can slowly turn the fish and bring them back to you. And watch the line, not the pole tips. When fishing real shallow, the fish will run off to the side. You will be able to see the line moving in a different direction long before you can see the pole tip move."

—Richard Williams,
Kentucky Lake crappie guide

A LESSON ABOUT SUPERSTRUCTURE

*S*tructure is a word often bandied about in crappie-fishing circles. A man named Buck Perry coined the term decades ago and defined it as "an unusual change in the bottom contour of a lake or river."

Since then, fishermen have used the word structure to describe almost any type of cover or bottom feature one might chance upon during a day of fishing. Fallen timber, brush piles, stumps, boat docks, riprap, weed-beds: you name it and someone will call it structure.

Savvy crappie anglers who want to catch lots of big slabs know structure is the place to find fish. Crappie are highly object-oriented and almost always found near some type of cover or bottom anomaly that might, in the loosest sense of the term, be called structure.

Crappie fans also popularized another term designed to increase an angler's chance of locating crappie. This word is *superstructure*. An understanding of superstructure can take any angler one step closer to success in the search for fish concentrations.

Superstructure is a smaller, specific component of much larger structure where crappie are likely to gather. For example, if a submerged creek channel on a lake bottom is structure, then superstructure might be a short, timbered point jutting into a bend on that channel. If a boat dock is structure, a brush pile or abrupt drop-off adjacent the dock might be superstructure.

Similarly, if a large underwater hump is structure, crappie won't be evenly dispersed all around the hump. Instead, they'll be attracted to areas such as an isolated cluster of stumps, a tall bushy snag or any other feature distinctly differ-

Many forms of superstructure can be seen in this photo of a lake that's been drawn down.

ent from the otherwise ordinary bottom feature. In other words, they're attracted to superstructure.

Lewis Peeler, a crappie fan from Vanndale, Arkansas, learned about superstructure on a spring crappie-fishing trip in Louisiana.

"A friend and I were jig fishing on a Mississippi River oxbow lake," he remembers. "A heavy rain had fallen the day prior to our arrival, and crappie were gathered in mid-lake areas around isolated cypress trees.

"There were several large solitary trees on the lake's north end, but crappie were not randomly scattered around them. We found the fish congregated in small, slightly deeper pockets of water situated near certain trees. We knew the crappie were probably in mid-lake haunts, but we had to refine our search to find the particular form of superstructure that attracted fish."

According to Peeler, fishing this lake was an important learning experience. "We'd work small tube jigs on one side of a tree and not get a nibble," he says. "Then we'd move them to the other side where our sonar indicated the water dropped abruptly from 4 to 6 feet. At that spot, we'd quickly catch a crappie. Prior to that day, before we understood the significance of superstructure, we might have jigged a few spots at a particular location then moved on, not realizing there were probably plenty of slabs nearby but holding only around certain parts of the structure we were fishing.

"I've seen virtually the same situation in expansive spreads of flooded dead timber on big Southern reservoirs like those managed by the U.S. Army Corps of Engineers," Peeler continues. "As is often the case, you fish several hours without catching anything and eventually decide you must be dealing with crappie that have a serious case of lockjaw. Then, in one specific location that looks the same as scores of others you've already tried, you hook and land a dandy crappie. You remove the hook, and as you're tossing the fish in the livewell, your fishing buddy casts a little spinner and another slab wallops his lure. You start thinking, thank

Arkansas angler Lewis Peeler caught this crappie and others on a subtle bit of superstructure—a bend in the creek channel running beneath the bridge in the background.

goodness they've started to bite. But likely as not, the crappie were biting all along. Up until this point, you just hadn't found them. They were holding near a small yet well-defined piece of superstructure. Perhaps there was a thick cluster of limbs still clinging to the side of one of the snags below the surface. Perhaps a different type of tree-created superstructure. If the flooded timber was comprised primarily of tall oaks and hickories, the bushy skeleton of a single cedar tree on one edge would probably draw heavy concentrations of crappie. Pinpoint the particular type of superstructure the crappie are using and you'll start landing them one after another."

Peeler's experience brings to mind a small lake where I often fish. The lake only covers about 20 acres, so it's easy to fish the entire body of water in a one-day outing. A row of cypress trees running through the lake's mid-section provides the only available crappie cover, except for one little pocket at the end of the cypress row where there's a dense stand of button willows.

I've never been able to resist the temptation to jig around all the cypress trees, and on each visit, I'll pick up a few nice crappie around the knees of those trees. When I think back, though, I realize I've probably wasted a lot of time fishing around the cypress trees because over half the crappie I've caught in that lake have come from within that patch of button willows.

The same phenomenon regarding tree types often applies to boat docks as well. Boat docks attract lots of crappie, but not all boat docks. Some are better than others,

A good fish finder is invaluable for pinpointing various types of superstructure that hold crappie.

and on lakes that have dozens of docks, the good docks might be considered a form of superstructure.

The docks most attractive to crappie are usually built on wood pilings, are in 5 to 15 feet of water near cover and/or structure, have been in the water several seasons and lie very close to the water's surface. Docks meeting these criteria are extremely attractive to crappie because they provide shade throughout the day. The wood pilings provide a comfortable sense of security, which structure-oriented crappie require, and they also harbor a smorgasbord of foods. Algae growing on the seasoned wood hide grass shrimp, newly hatched minnows, aquatic insects, insect larvae and other crappie favorites.

Size is another consideration. Think of docks as fish hotels. Big hotels have rooms for lots of guests. Occupancy is limited, though, at smaller establishments. If other traits are equal, concentrate on large docks.

If you have a sonar unit on your boat, be sure to watch for brush piles placed around docks by the owners or local anglers. It's a rare instance when there aren't several brush piles in the vicinity, and rare, too, when you won't find several nice crappie hiding within each of these shelters. Look, too, for nuances in bottom structure near docks that might concentrate fish—creek channels, deep pockets, small humps or other features.

Crappie anglers also should learn to distinguish between *in-structures* and *out-structures*. In-structures are always connected to the shore; out-structures are away from the shore, often in mid-lake or mid-stream.

One example of in-structure for crappie would be a long grassy point that gradually slopes into deeper water. A tree that has become uprooted and fallen over

Making a distinction between in-structures, like a shallow grassy point (left) and out-structures such as bridge piers (right) can increase an angler's catch. Crappie generally use in-structures in spring and fall and out-structures in summer and winter.

into the water would be in-structure, as would a fishing pier or anything else that is clearly part of the shoreline.

Out-structures include features such as bridge piers, inundated stream channels, humps, inundated ponds, saddles between islands, man-made fish attractors, timbered bars or any similar bottom feature well away from the shoreline.

The most important difference between these two fishing areas is that crappie generally use in-structures in spring and fall and out-structures in summer and winter. The only time crappie travel any appreciable distance is when they're making seasonal migrations from in-structures to out-structures or vice versa.

"This is important for crappie fisherman to know," says Peeler. "Each bit of superstructure where you find crappie should, if it remains unchanged, always attract crappie. But in most cases, crappie will only be found on that particular piece of superstructure during the proper season—on in-structure in spring and fall, on out-structure in summer and winter.

"You should still concentrate your attention on superstructure regardless of the season," he notes. "For example, if I'm fishing in-structure during the spring spawning season, I'll look for something slightly different on the main structure that will concentrate crappie. A patch of green buckbrush may contain a log or cluster of stumps that draws crappie. If I'm fishing a brushy cove, I'll look for small points or other features along the perimeter where crappie are likely to hold. If I find crappie scattered here and there around cypress trees, I'll watch for unusual stands of trees that might tend to keep crappie more tightly schooled—trees in slightly deeper water or trees more tightly bunched together, things like that.

"Likewise, if I'm fishing around out-structure during summer and winter, I focus my attention on superstructure that shows up on my fish finder," he continues. "Primary creek channels are among the best structures to fish during these seasons, but crappie won't be found along the entire length of each channel. Instead, they'll be gathered in spots where the channel exhibits a change of some sort. This may be a bit of cover where a secondary channel intersects the main channel, or around a tall tree standing on a sharp bend in the channel—anything different from the norm. Finding these types of superstructure can mean the difference between catching lots of crappie or none at all."

Every good crappie fisherman knows the fundamentals of structure fishing. But if you want to improve your success rate even more, learn how to find and fish superstructure. This refined form of structure fishing will become the foundation for some of the best crappie fishing you've ever enjoyed.

UNDERSTANDING OXBOWS

Word has it the crappie are tearing it up on a nearby oxbow lake. All week, a friend at the pool hall has been bragging about the cooler full of crappie he caught last Saturday. The fishing report in yesterday's newspaper said several 2-pounders were weighed in earlier this week, and limit stringers have been common.

You heard similar reports this time last year but never found time to make the long drive. No such misfortune now, though, so you hitch up the boat, pick up your fishing pal Bubba, and at dawn, the two of you have your first glimpse of this 1,000-acre natural lake.

Everything looks perfect. It's been raining to the north for several days, but the skies here are just overcast. You're a bit surprised there aren't more folks out fishing, but, hey, that just makes things all the better.

As the sun sets, you arrive back at the boat ramp. "I just don't understand it," Bubba whines. "Just a few days ago, Mack was over here and loaded the boat with some dandy crappie. We get here and nothing . . . not even a nibble."

Oxbow lakes offer excellent crappie fishing in incredibly scenic settings.

Has something similar to this ever happened to you? For many inexperienced anglers, catching crappie in an oxbow lake is like attempting to break a secret code. Try as they might, it seems impossible to achieve success, and many go away frustrated, vowing never again to fish an oxbow.

Contrary to the opinions of some unfortunate fishermen, the only real secret to oxbow crappie fishing is preparing yourself with an in-depth knowledge of oxbow dynamics. In many physical respects, oxbows are vastly different than man-made lakes, and each oxbow has characteristics that make it different from other oxbows. Unless one knows and understands these differences, fishing for crappie may be nothing more than a water haul.

What the fellows in our opening story didn't know was upstate rains had caused the adjoining river to overflow into the oxbow forty-eight hours prior to their arrival. Yes, folks were catching lots of crappie a few days earlier, and by all appearances, it should have been a decent day for fishing. But a sharp rise in the water level, unnoticeable to our fishing duo, gave the crappie a bad case of lockjaw. Few fishermen were on the lake that day because most regulars knew of the impending rise and knew crappie weren't likely to bite until conditions stabilized.

Rapidly changing water levels are just one of several factors oxbow anglers must figure into the crappie-angling equation. To better understand the variables that influence oxbow crappie fishing, let's examine the origins and physical attributes of oxbow lakes. Knowing what to look for, and when and where, will increase your odds for success.

Oxbow Origins

A lowland river left to its own devices will writhe and twist in its valley like a head-shot snake. The river erodes earth away in one place only to deposit it somewhere else, and though a river may always look the same to a casual visitor, it's never the same two days in a row.

Over the years, a lowland river plows a new channel here and aban-

Many small oxbow lakes have limited access and thus little fishing pressure. Crappie grow huge as a result.

dons an old one there, always following the path of least resistance. Sometimes, when a meandering stream erodes the shores of its broad bends, loops of water are severed from the main stream. The ends of the loops are blocked by sediments deposited by the parent stream, and a crescent-shaped lake is left behind. The shape of these lakes resembles the U-shaped piece of wood on an ox yoke, and thus they are called oxbow lakes. Oxbow lakes are also known as cutoffs or river lakes.

When an oxbow is cut off from the river, its character immediately begins changing. The absence of continually flowing water allows sediment carried in from seasonal flooding to build up on the bottom, and the old meander scar becomes shallower and relatively flat-bottomed. Water-tolerant plants such as cypress, tupelos and willows take root along the lake's edges. In years of drought, some shallow oxbows dry up, allowing plants to gain a foothold and encroach still farther into the lake. It's because of this cyclic process that many oxbows have large cypress trees growing in the middle of the lake, or have a ring of living trees and shrubs extending 50 to 100 feet or more out from dry land.

All these natural processes, from the natural cutting off of a new oxbow to the building up of bottom sediment to the gradual extension of woody vegetation farther and farther from the bank, are stages in the death of an oxbow lake. The process may take 500 years or more, but left undisturbed, all oxbows eventually silt in and transform into wetland forest.

During this long process of dying, oxbows can provide fantastic crappie fishing. The annual cycle of winter/spring flooding that gradually chokes these lakes with silt also figures heavily in making them the outstanding crappie fisheries they are.

The annual flooding cycle stimulates oxbow crappie to go on a feeding binge as waters recede to normal levels. The feeding binge puts them in excellent spawning condition, and because oxbows are very fertile, heavy spawns usually follow each winter/spring flooding cycle. Spawning still occurs in years of low rain, when flooding is absent, but it doesn't happen with the gusto that characterizes post-flood spawns.

Oxbow Types

Mastering oxbow crappie fishing requires knowledge of the various types of oxbow lakes. Some oxbows remain connected to the parent stream; some are not. Some lie within the floodplain of major streams, while others lie entirely outside the floodplain. Differing conditions on each type of oxbow dictate the manner and amount of planning necessary to enjoy a productive crappie-fishing trip.

Oxbows that remain connected to their parent river during all or part of the year normally provide the best fishing for big crappie. When the connecting river

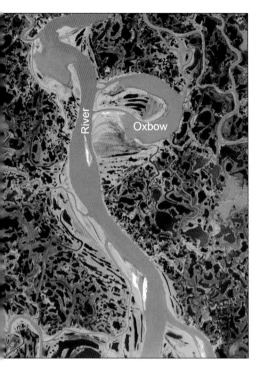

floods the oxbow, inflowing nutrients enrich the water and help sustain thriving communities of forage animals on which crappie feed. This yearly overflow cycle also provides temporary, but important, spawning habitat for oxbow crappie.

Unfortunately, severe water-level fluctuations also make river-connected oxbows the trickiest to fish. When the river rises to a certain level, the lake also rises. When the river falls, the lake falls. Changing water conditions dramatically affect fishing, and anglers must monitor water levels closely to pick the most productive days.

There are no hard-and-fast rules for fishing river-connected oxbows; fish are caught under all conditions. But as a general rule, crappie seldom bite when the water is on a fast rise. Fishing run-out areas—the cuts connecting oxbow and river—can sometimes be outstanding during a fast fall. But the best fishing on these oxbows is usually when the water level is steady or slowly rising or falling.

On river-connected oxbows, crappie anglers also should know the depth at which the river moves in and out of the oxbow being fished. This information is usually available at local bait shops or from area anglers. When you know it, you can monitor the river level in local newspapers or via government hotlines or websites to plan a trip during peak fishing periods. When the river is entirely out of the oxbow, water conditions, and thus fishing conditions, are likely to be more stable and predictable. When the river overflows into the oxbow, anglers must know the intensity of water level fluctuations—fast rise, slow fall, etc.—to determine the best crappie fishing days.

Many oxbows are no longer connected to the river proper but still lie within the stream floodplain. These lakes are still subject to flooding and rapidly changing water levels during wet months, and here again, crappie anglers should scrutinize water fluctuations when planning a visit.

Some oxbows lie outside the river floodplain, completely isolated by levees or dams. These lakes usually provide the most predictable fishing opportunities because water fluctuations are less dramatic and have less influence on overall fishing conditions. Consequently, they may be the best oxbows to fish when water conditions are unfavorable elsewhere. If it's big crappie you seek, however, you'll probably be disappointed. The absence of an annual overflow cycle leads to decreased fertility, and quality crappie—1-1/2- to 3-pounders—are seldom found.

These general guidelines can be helpful, but don't neglect to do additional homework before fishing. Some isolated oxbows offer astounding fishing for trophy-class crappie, and some river-connected lakes may produce few, if any, crappie. Prepare yourself by contacting local bait-shop proprietors or fisheries biologists and asking a few basic questions. Is this a good crappie lake during this time of year? What size crappie are likely to be caught? Can you offer pointers on picking the best fishing days? Can you suggest where I might call for an up-to-date report on fishing conditions? The more you know about a lake before you visit, the better your chances for success.

Finding Oxbow Crappie

Finding oxbow crappie isn't unusually complicated. Work all available cover carefully, probing every nook and cranny in the brush and every likely log, stump and cypress tree, changing baits and presentations until you find what works best.

One thing to remember is that even though most oxbows are relatively flat and of uniform depth, the outside bend of the lake is almost always a little deeper than the inside bend. This can be important when water temperatures rise above the crappie's 70- to 75-degree comfort range. When this happens, crappie tend to concentrate on the lake's deeper side where the temperature is more to their liking. In most oxbows, the amount of deep water is very limited, so you don't have to look far to find fish.

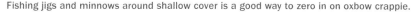

Fishing jigs and minnows around shallow cover is a good way to zero in on oxbow crappie.

When crappie are in the shallows, they invariably relate to some sort of cover. Cypress trees are prevalent in many oxbows, and using a long pole to work jigs or minnows around their broad bases and knees often is a good way to catch crappie.

If the fish are skittish, and it is difficult to approach close enough to use a pole without spooking them, try a tactic Southern anglers call stump-knocking. Remain at a distance, and use an ultralight spinning or spincast combo to cast a jig or jig/spinner combo right up against the side of the tree. Cast right at the tree, and let the lure smack into the trunk and roll off into the water below. Crappie usually hold right beside the tree in hollows and folds, waiting to ambush passing baitfish or watching for insects to tumble off the branches overhead. Most will strike as soon as the lure tumbles into the water, but if you don't get a hit right away, retrieve the lure and try other spots.

Buckbrush and willows also are prevalent in many oxbows, and many crappie are caught in the thickest such cover available. Other prime fishing spots include fallen trees, beaver lodges, sunken Christmas-tree shelters, lily pads, weed-beds, shoreline riprap, stump fields, boat docks and duck-hunting blinds.

If you're on an oxbow when flood waters are receding, try fishing around run-out chutes between oxbow and river. These are crappie magnets that attract fish with the promise of an easy meal. Look for areas where out-flowing water is constricted, such as sloughs and natural cuts, then work a minnow, jig or jig/spinner combo around surrounding woody cover. Key your efforts to periods when water is falling 3 to 6 inches a day; a faster fall makes it hard to locate fish.

One final note: when you're considering where to go, think small. Although some oxbows cover several thousand acres, the real jewels are much smaller. It's harder to pinpoint crappie in the larger oxbows, and fishing these lakes isn't much different than fishing the nearest Corps of Engineers mega-lake.

The run-out chute between an oxbow lake and its parent river often is a crappie magnet.

For the true oxbow experience, visit small lakes off the beaten path. It's not uncommon to fish all day on one of these little oxbows and never see another boat. The splendid bottomland scenery will take you back to a time when our country was still wild and uncharted, and you'll experience a feeling of wonderment and tranquility no man-made impoundment can impart. When the crappie are biting, there's only one way to describe it: heaven on earth.

Understanding oxbow lakes and how to fish them will add a whole new dimension to your fishing. Hopefully, the facts presented here will help you get off to a good start, so you, too, can enjoy the magic and majesty of these blue-ribbon crappie lakes.

KEEP IT SIMPLE

Simplicity is the watchword for oxbow-fishing success. Some oxbows encompass 1,000 acres or more, with launching facilities for even large bass boats. Most, however, cover 100 acres or less, with primitive launch sites. Lightweight johnboats or canoes are ideal fishing craft, and on small oxbows, an outboard is unnecessary. Bring a sculling paddle.

Tackle also should be simple. Crappie anglers use cane poles, jigging poles or ultralight combos. Jigs, minnows and jig/minnow combos are preferred crappie baits, though some anglers also do well fishing spinners and small crankbaits.

OXBOW FISH POPULATION DYNAMICS

Many oxbow fishermen believe the annual flooding cycle in river-connected oxbows is actually a restocking process, with floodwaters bringing in a new batch of crappie each year. But telemetry and netting studies have proven this isn't so. There's enough fish movement from river to lake or from one lake to another to restore a fish population to an oxbow that has dried up over a hot summer, but the mass influx of catchable-size crappie that many anglers envision simply doesn't occur.

What happens is, annual floods stimulate the existing fish population in a river-bottom oxbow to go on a feeding binge. The feeding binge puts them in excellent spawning condition, and because the oxbows are so fertile, heavy spawns usually follow each winter/spring flooding cycle. Increased hatches of fry lead to increased numbers of catchable-size crappie.

CATCHING CRAPPIE IN MUDDY WATERS

One of my favorite crappie-fishing spots is a remote lake in a big, bottomland national wildlife refuge. My friends and I call it Lake Jekyll and Hyde because it has two very different personalities.

From summer through fall, the lake holds clear water. Tannins give the lake an iced-tea tint, but the water is clearer than the Lipton's you make at home.

During most years, however, Jekyll-and-Hyde undergoes a dramatic transformation in winter. A nearby river rises and spills into the lake, bringing silt and debris with it. The lake becomes very muddy. ("You could track a coon across it," one of my buddies says.) And it usually stays muddy until summer.

All this might not matter if Jekyll-and-Hyde wasn't swarming with 2-pound-plus crappie. But it is, and my fishing pals and I find it hard to stay away very long. We fish the lake year-round, and that being the case, we've had to learn how to catch crappie in muddy water and clear.

At first, we avoided the lake when it was muddy. It didn't seem possible sight-feeders like crappie could ever find a bait in water as thick and dark as hot chocolate. We were wrong, though. Crappie will bite in muddy water, and if you know a few tips for finding and enticing them in these silty environs, you may catch more fish than you ever have in clear waters. Now that we've learned that, we spend more days fishing Lake Hyde and fewer days fishing Lake Jekyll. Experience has shown muddy water equals more crappie when you know what to do.

Understanding the Effects of Muddy Water

All sorts of crappie waters experience high levels of turbidity. Some stay muddy year-round; others get muddy only after periods of rain and run-off, or during the turbulence of fall turnover.

Muddy water and clear. A jig hangs in each container. Surely most anglers would say they prefer fishing in transparent water like that on the right. But muddy-water fishing isn't as hard as it might seem if you learn a few tricks.

Crappie hold very close to cover objects in murky water. The angler may need to slide a jig right down the wood to catch them.

When you first confront muddy-water conditions, you may wonder if it's worthwhile to try fishing. Rest assured, however, crappie don't quit feeding because the water lacks clarity. Crappie in turbid water eat as often as when water is clearer. To catch them, however, you must use special fishing tactics.

Muddy water is like a night with dense fog. Visibility is extremely limited. Just as ship captains must rely on radar rather than sight to navigate under such conditions, sight becomes of secondary importance to crappie. As visibility decreases, the fish rely more on sound, vibrations and odor to find their meals.

Muddy-water crappie also are likely to be in shallower habitats because oxygen levels are better in the shallows. Additionally, muddy-water crappie usually hold very tight against woody cover features. This apparently gives them a reference point and a sense of security when visibility is poor. They're usually mere inches away from features such as snags, stumps, stick-ups and the like.

Keep in mind, too, fishing for muddy-water crappie may actually be best on sunny days. Under other conditions, the early morning and evening hours may be best. But in opaque waters, midday hours may be most productive.

One Angler's Solutions

Steve Filipek is a fisheries biologist with the Arkansas Game and Fish Commission. He's tackled muddy-water fishing conditions often during a lifetime of crappie fishing. He notes that crappie prefer the least muddy water they can find, and looking for more favorable water conditions is the first step to finding fish.

"If the water I'm fishing is muddy, the first thing I do is look for places where the water is just a little clearer—up in creeks, the backs of coves, around beds of green vegetation, places like that," he says. "Crappie are sight feeders, and even the slightest bit of clearer water improves the chance of them seeing your bait.

"You also should remember that crappie hold much tighter to cover when the water's muddy," Filipek reports. "Most of us fish an area quickly, then move to the next spot. But in muddy water, you have to be more patient. Cover the whole 360 degrees around that stump or treetop, and do it much slower than you normally would. Work your bait close to the cover, work it slowly, and be thorough."

Though he's primarily a jig fisherman, Filipek also keeps a supply of minnows for muddy-water fishing. "It's a good idea to carry live minnows on all your trips," he says. "In muddy water, crappie can home in on a minnow's scent and vibrations. A jig tipped with a minnow may out-produce a plain jig, so I often try that if fishing is tough."

As water visibility decreases, crappie move to shallow water. According to Filipek, this is another fact many crappie anglers overlook.

"In muddy lakes, I've seen crappie so shallow their fins were coming out of the water," he says. "So I concentrate my fishing close to the banks.

"Catching crappie in muddy water isn't as hard as you'd think," he continues. "In fact, I'm not sure it affects fish as much as it affects fishermen. Be patient, present your lure right in front of them, and you'll usually find crappie eager to bite."

To get the most from your fishing when water is murky, it helps to know some tips for success. Here are some to get you started.

Enticements

Live minnows always are superb crappie baits, but their benefits really shine when fishing muddy water. Crappie quickly zero in on a baitfish's scent, and because minnows can be fished stationary close to cover, you can place them right under the fish's noses.

Working a jig right beside wood cover such as stumps, snags and logs is another way to catch muddy-water crappie. Put the lure on the wood and let it slide down, maintaining contact with the wood as you fish. In this situation, crappie often are close enough to touch the wood, which gives them a sense of security.

In silty water, light penetrates less, and colors on the darker end of the spectrum are more easily seen by crappie. Thus, darker-colored jigs—black, purple, dark blue, etc.—often produce more strikes than colors such as red, yellow and chartreuse.

Because crappie in muddy water rely more on sound and vibrations to find food, it also may prove helpful to enhance your jigs for more acoustical attraction. A small rattle pushed into the jig body may help, or glue plastic "wobbly eyes" to each side of the jig head. Adding a scent product or using soft-plastic jig bodies that contain

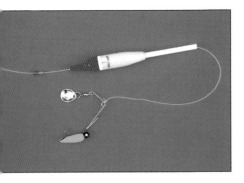

To fish a spinner at the slow speed often needed in muddy water, it helps to add a sliding bobber above the lure.

fish attractants (Yum's Wooly Beavertail and Mister Twister's Exude Curly Tail Grub are good ones) can improve the effectiveness of jigs even more.

I also like fishing spinners in muddy water. Flash and vibration make these lures easier for crappie to find, and spinners are ideal for working shallows where crappie usually hold.

My favorites are safety-pin spinners such as the Johnson Beetle-Spin, but it's difficult to fish them at the snail's pace often needed. To combat this problem, I rig a slip bobber above the lure. Place a bobber stop on your line at the depth you want to fish. Then add a bead below the stop, followed by the slip bobber. Finish the rig by tying on the spinner. This rig lets you slow your presentation and keep the spinner in the strike zone. Use a variety of retrieves—small twitches, a slow, steady retrieve or long pulls with a few seconds of motionlessness between—until you determine a good pattern.

Problems with waters muddy enough to "track a coon across" need not hamper your fishing success. In fact, crappie fishing in murky waters can work to the savvy angler's advantage. The knowledgeable fisherman will almost always find crappie eager to bite, regardless of water clarity.

So next time you're on a body of water so muddy it seems like your boat has run aground, don't fret. Settle in, put your knowledge of muddy-water fishing tactics to work, and start reeling in those slabs.

LOCATIONAL TIPS

Catching crappie in muddy water may require frequent moves to find the best fishing locales. The following facts may help you pinpoint fish:

- If the water is high and muddy when fishing a big river system for crappie, do some scouting to pinpoint good fishing locales. High water lets you get back into chutes, cuts and backwaters off the river, places you may not have noticed before. And while you're up in these areas, you may find that water off the main river is clearer and easier to fish. If you find the right spot, it could turn a bad fishing day into a good one.

- On windy days, light penetration falls. On calm days, light penetrates further. Keep this in mind even when fishing muddy waters. You may have to adjust the depth you fish by a foot or two as conditions change. Work shallower in wind and a bit deeper during periods of calm.
- When fishing where water is turbid, watch what happens to the water when you turn on your trolling motor. If it changes color around the prop, the water below the surface is clearer and you may catch more crappie by fishing deeper.

COPING WITH CLEAR WATER

At times, crappie anglers must learn to cope with exceptionally clear water conditions that make it difficult to catch crappie. For example, in-flows from clear creeks and lakes lend a transparency to the water that enables sight-feeding crappie to discern anything out of place in their environment. Crappie-fishing efforts may prove virtually fruitless unless the angler can adapt.

To help overcome problems associated with clear-water fishing, remember these tips:

- Use lighter line (4-pound instead of 8, for instance) that's harder for crappie to detect.
- When possible, make long casts, remaining some distance from the cover you're fishing, so you're not as likely to frighten fish.
- When the sun is high, crappie move deeper to avoid bright light. But in early morning and late afternoon, light penetration is minimal, and crappie move to shallower, near-shore waters to feed, making them easier to find. Cloudy or windy days are good, too.
- If shady cover is available, clear-water crappie may stay in fairly shallow water throughout the day. Investigate flooded thickets,

When water is crystal clear, adaptive anglers still can catch crappie.

channels beneath bridges, underwater ledges, boat docks (especially those built close to the water) and floating log jams. Virtually anything that casts a shadow is potentially productive.

- Minnows may outproduce artificials in clear water because there's nothing phony for crappie to observe. When using artificials, use smaller versions and a fast retrieve. Don't give crappie time to inspect them.

PRO TIP

"Muddy water usually warms up quicker than clear water, so crappie in muddy water may be feeding more actively. We catch a lot of them on flats near creek channels close to spawning areas by spider trolling with eight 12-foot B'n'M poles rigged with 6-pound Vicious HiVis line. Each pole is outfitted with one of B'n'M's Capps & Coleman Minnow Rigs, but we replace the bottom hook with a chartreuse or orange  Blakemore Pro Series Road Runner head tipped with a live minnow. This Road Runner's willow blade gives it extra flash that helps in muddy water. And the HiVis line allows us to detect more bites we might otherwise miss."

—Crappie pros Jim and Barbara Reedy, Charleston, Missouri

PRO TIP

"My favorite crappie lakes often are high and muddy in spring. During this time, I like to use a large bait that glows—a 1/8-ounce Bobby Garland Mo'Glo jighead with a Mo'Glo Stroll'R jig tied with a basic loop knot. I have a 3/16-ounce bullet weight with two round split shot clamped 18 inches above the jig. This rig is slow-trolled in upper parts of the water column. The lure's action and glow help crappie locate and attack it even when visibility is limited."

—Mississippi crappie pro Brad Chappell

SWAMP CRAPPIE

It's a pleasant afternoon, but a chill runs up my spine. It's not the temperature that causes me to shiver, however. It's alligators.

The huge reptiles are all around us, calling out in baritone voices. I can hear at least five bellowing from different places, yet I cannot see any. They're totally hidden in the dense vegetation of the swamp, and that makes me uneasy.

I wonder what might happen if the boat swamped and we were forced to swim to shore. The mere thought makes my hair stand on end.

Whitey Outlaw and I are sitting in his boat in a remote corner of South Carolina's Lake Marion, one of the famed Santee-Cooper lakes. For Whitey, this is home water. He's fished here all his life and knows the 110,000-acre lake like a country boy knows his favorite farm pond. That's a good thing, I decide, because right now I'm as lost as a goose.

Around us, as far as we can see, are cypress trees and floating mats of water hyacinth, gator grass and duckweed. The vegetation on the water's surface is so close-knit, it appears you could step out of the boat and walk in any direction as far as you might wish. In reality, the surface weeds are only a blanket. The water beneath the plants is several feet deep. A stroll is out of the question, even if there weren't alligators.

Gators there are, however, and lots of other wildlife, too. A water snake slithers past the boat. Overhead, ospreys and anhingas are bringing fish to their young in treetop nests. Turtles bask on logs. Herons and egrets stand like sentinels in the shallows.

No doubt, any naturalist would enjoy a visit here. But for most people, Stumphole Swamp (that's what the locals call it) is no more inviting than a spooky old mansion on Halloween. It looks forbidding, and it is.

It's definitely not what you picture when you think about crappie fishing, either. But that's the reason Whitey has brought me here. He wants to show me a unique angling method he and fishing partner Dean Sanders use to catch the crappie swimming Lake Marion's backwaters.

Floating mats of water hyacinth, gator grass and other vegetation may appear unfishable, but open a hole to the water beneath, and it's often possible to pull out a nice crappie.

Swamps are full of wildlife, including alligators.

For starters, Whitey shows me the brute-force method one must use to reach the dark, swampy recesses he and Dean like to fish. Sitting in open water at the edge of the weed-beds, he revs his outboard and then goes barreling through the dense cover, full speed ahead. As we wheel this way and that through the maze of cypress trees, I realize alligators aren't the only threat to life and limb.

When the short boat ride ends and I open my eyes, we're buried in the swamp and Whitey's on his feet fishing.

"Crappie fishing this way isn't for everybody," he says as he works a long jig pole through the cover to a tiny hole beside a cypress. "A man who likes open water has no business here. He'll have a nervous breakdown."

I hold my knees down to make them quit shaking and watch as Whitey deftly drops a jig into a hole the size of a coffee mug and gives it a little flip.

No bite is forthcoming, and Whitey doesn't wait for one. He backs the pole out, weaves it through the brush in a different spot and then drops the jig in another hole even smaller than the first. This time, his pole bows, and he sets the hook with an upward snap. He grabs the line with one hand, pulls the fish snug against the pole tip and backs the rig into the boat so he can remove his catch. It's a black crappie, pretty as a piece of silver jewelry.

We don't stay in this spot long. Whitey starts the outboard and guns it again, moving us even deeper into the swamp. The vegetation we motor through is as tangled as a backlash in a baitcaster, but the johnboat passes through surprisingly easy. As soon as we stop, Whitey's up and fishing again, dropping his jig in little openings most anglers would never think might hold crappie.

"I caught a good one right by this tree a few days ago," he says, holding the jig beside

Whitey Outlaw brings a weed-bed crappie into the boat while fishing the dense vegetation of South Carolina's Lake Marion.

the knee of a cypress. "After you fish here awhile, you learn there are certain places that almost always produce a fish or two. You catch one here, one there, keeping on the move and hitting all your good spots.

"The best fishing is when the water is about the same color as a brown paper bag," he continues. "My favorite months are October, November and December, then again from early March through mid-April."

The reason this sort of fishing is so good, Whitey tells me, is other folks never venture into these swampy areas. Earlier, as we motored across the main lake, we passed boats full of anglers. Each boat was less than a stone's throw away from another, and there were dozens.

"I don't like fishing where there are so many people," Whitey said. "That's why I like getting back into the swamp, away from the edges. You never see anyone else, and the crappie fishing is far better than it is in more open areas that get pounded by every passing angler."

Whitey Outlaw (left) and Dean Sanders appear stranded in a bed of hyacinth, but they're preparing to fish for crappie in the water beneath the dense, floating mat of vegetation. Dean (right) is using a conduit pole to open a fishing hole in the weeds.

Our next wild boat run takes us close to another boat, nevertheless. It's Dean Sanders, Whitey's longtime fishing companion, and my friend Mark Shealy.

"Catching any?" I holler.

"A few," Dean says, holding up a nice crappie.

Dean lives in Cope, South Carolina. Whitey lives in St. Matthews. The two are among the country's most respected crappie pros. They've won many major tournaments, including several Crappie USA and Crappie Masters events.

Slow trolling jigs, long lining and trolling crankbaits are among their preferred crappie-fishing techniques, but the number one tactic on their list of favorites is vertical jigging vegetation in the manner Whitey has spent the past hour showing me.

"This is far and away my favorite method for catching crappie," Dean says after motoring his boat to the middle of a big hyacinth patch.

Whitey and Mark have swapped places, so Mark and I can watch the Sanders/Outlaw Swamp Fishing Show. An interesting show it is.

Dean pulls a long metal pole from the boat and starts scratching a hole in the floating mat of vegetation.

"It's made from thin, 1/2-inch conduit," Whitey says. "Ten feet long with a 12-inch, 90-degree bend on the end."

Dean pokes the bent end in the weeds and moves it about to create a small opening. Whitey, standing at the ready, drops in a jig and quickly pulls out a crappie.

I've read about a similar technique used to fish weed-beds on Florida lakes. Anglers use a rake to create big openings—sometimes several feet across—in weed-beds. As the plants are moved, grass shrimp, insect larvae and other invertebrates are stirred up. These small forage animals attract baitfish, which in turn attract crappie.

Dean Sanders appears buried in cover as he jigs for swamp crappie.

The method used by Whitey and Dean, however, creates only a very small opening. "About the size of a five-gallon bucket or less," Whitey says. Their method also creates a chain reaction in the food chain, but it's main function is to create openings where the men can drop jigs to the numerous crappie below. The crappie already are feeding there. Dean and Whitey just need a way to get to them.

A crappie pole used by the duo was developed by Whitey specifically for this type of fishing. Called the Whitey Outlaw Series Santee Elite, it's manufactured by B'n'M Poles. This pole has no guides or eyes and features a line-through-the-blank design. This allows more aggressive fishing in heavy vegetation because there are no guides to get hung in brush. The two-section, 100-percent graphite poles are available in 10-, 11- and 12-foot models.

"The line we use is Berkley Trilene Solar," says Whitey. "Usually we spool up with 8-pound-test, but if the cover is really thick, we may go as heavy as 10-pound."

"The jigs we use are made by Southern Pro Tackle and Mid-South Tackle," Dean adds. "For this kind of fishing, we prefer 1-1/2-inch, 1/16-ounce jigs. We switch colors until we figure out what the crappie want on the day we're fishing."

Add all this together—the right tackle and the right technique in the right place—and you have a deadly combination for fall crappie. Whitey and Dean prove it's so by landing several more nice crappie while I snap photos.

As I watch the pair fishing, I'm struck by how unusual the scene is. From our vantage point, it looks like Dean and Whitey are a couple of crazy men who've somehow run their boat onto someone's overgrown yard and started fishing. No water is visible—just two anglers, a boat and acres of thick weeds.

As if to prove they're not crazy, however, Whitey sets the hook in a nice largemouth and holds it up for Mark and me to see.

"That's another thing I love about this kind of fishing," Whitey hollers. "You never know what's gonna bite next."

What does bite next is a snake. We watch as Whitey sets the hook. Then when he swings his long, squirming catch over the transom, we watch as Dean darts to the other end of the boat to avoid the serpent.

"Like I said," Whitey shouts. "You never know what's gonna bite next. You just hope it doesn't bite you!"

That's swamp fishing for you—lots of snakes and lots of alligators, but also lots of jumbo crappie. It's certainly not for everyone, but if you give Whitey and Dean's weed-bed fishing tactics a try, chances are you'll be catching crappie when other folks are just trying. Give it a shot this season and see.

SWAMP FISHING LOCALES

Want to give swamp fishing a try but don't know where to go?

My home state of Arkansas encompasses some of the biggest swamps in the country, including the Big Woods area, stretching along the White and Cache rivers, which includes hundreds of thousands of acres punctuated with scores of oxbow lakes, bayous and backwaters full of crappie. Swamps occur throughout much of our country, from New Jersey and Indiana to Texas and Florida. Many are protected as national wildlife refuges or wildlife management areas, such as Okefenokee Swamp in Georgia and Florida, Honey Island Swamp in Louisiana and Mingo Swamp in Missouri. And most serve up excellent fishing for crappie. A call to your state fisheries agency should help you find a swamp you can explore and fish on your own.

CRANKIN' UP SUMMER SLABS

Hang around this country's top crappie anglers and you'll learn something that may surprise you. During summer, when crappie move to deeper haunts, many of these anglers don't fish with jigs, minnows, spinners or other baits you might expect. Instead, they use crankbaits to entice hot-weather slabs.

Most of them aren't just chunking and winding one crankbait, either. These expert fishermen troll with multi-pole set-ups, using as many as sixteen crankbaits simultaneously.

Why crankbaits? Three primary reasons are cited by every crankbait aficionado. First, crankbaits quickly reach the strike zone and stay there, allowing you to thoroughly work the band of water where summer fish are likely to be. Second, with crankbaits, you can cover lots of water quickly to find scattered summer crappie schools. And third, crankbaits are excellent big-fish lures. Smaller fish also hit cranks, but crappie 1-1/2 pounds and larger, which often refuse smaller offerings, rarely ignore a crankbait.

If you want to try crankbaits, here are some tried-and-true tactics from pro anglers that can help you nab slabs this season.

The Rebel Deep Wee-R crankbait is the favorite of Alabama crappie guide Brad Whitehead when targeting big summer slabs like this. PHOTO COURTESY OF Brad Whitehead

Some anglers never fish crankbaits on multiple poles because it seems too difficult. But Brad Whitehead, seen fishing here with the author's wife, Theresa Sutton, says learning this tactic is easy, and using it can put lots of summer slabs in the boat.

Brad Whitehead: The Sixteen-Pole Man

Brad Whitehead of Muscle Shoals, Alabama, a member of B'n'M Poles Pro Staff, is a crappie guide on Wilson and Pickwick lakes. When trolling crankbaits for crappie, he's a sixteen-pole man.

"I troll with four poles in front, four on the sides and eight in back, which helps me catch more crappie," he says. "Some folks think this would be really difficult, but it's not. And the more water you can cover, the more crappie you'll find."

Whitehead's favorite crankbait is Rebel's 3/8-ounce Deep Wee-R, a 2-inch minnow imitation that dives 8 to 10 feet.

"I sometimes replace the No. 6 hooks with red, No. 4 Gamakatsu round-bend trebles," he says. "My favorite lure colors are blue/chartreuse, black/chartreuse and brown crawdad. I troll with lures in all three colors until fish show a preference, and then change all rigs to match that preference until the pattern changes."

The poles Whitehead uses are all from B'n'M. They're positioned in Driftmaster and Hi-Tek Stuff rod holders as follows: four 13-foot Black Widow poles out the front rack, one 14-foot and one 12-foot Pro-Staff Trolling Rod on each side (14 in front of 12) and eight 6-1/2-foot Buck's Graphite Spinning Rods out the back. He prefers Pflueger light spinning reels or baitcasters spooled with Shakespeare Supreme 6- to 8-pound-test.

"Low-pound-test line is a must for this type of fishing," he says. "And you need a GPS to maintain the proper boat speed when trolling."

Whitehead rigs crankbaits one of two ways. At times, he simply connects the crankbait to a snap swivel on his line and trolls the lure 60 to 70 yards behind the boat. But when crappie are on deeper structures, he adds a 3- to 5-ounce egg sinker. The sinker is on the line above a barrel swivel, then a 3-foot crankbait leader is attached to the swivel's other eye.

"The sinker rig is like a Carolina rig," he says. "It pulls the crankbait into deeper water it normally can't reach. With it, I may use heavier line that doesn't abrade or hang up as much. I like this rig because not only do you catch monster crappie, you also catch saugers and walleyes."

Most crappie Whitehead catches on unweighted crankbaits are on flats near river and creek channels.

"Mornings are best for flats fishing," he notes. "Then, as the sun gets higher, crappie move to deeper water on channel edges. That's when weighted crankbaits really shine.

"I make a long cast with each pole, then just watch my graph and GPS and go," he continues. "I start trolling at 1.5 mph. Speed is very important. When you get locked in at the right pace, your day will be full of papermouths. And with crankbaits, those are likely to be big fish—13 to 15 inches or more. You won't catch a limit that size every day, but on average, more than half your catch will be big slabs."

Kent Driscoll: Eight Poles, Eight Lures

Kent Driscoll of Cordova, Tennessee, a longtime avid crappie angler, has fished professional crappie circuits many years and is a member of B'n'M Poles' Pro Staff. One of his specialties is catching summer crappie on crankbaits.

"On the lakes I fish, the summer crankbait pattern starts when the water temperature hits 80 degrees," he says. "I look for the thermocline to determine the depth of the fish. Most crappie suspend at 10 to 15 feet in water 20 to 40 feet deep. I focus on fishing deep flats, major river ledges and channels."

Driscoll fishes with Bandit crankbaits, particularly the 300 Series. He also uses 2-3/8-inch, Series 3 Yo-Zuri Hardcore Crankbaits.

"Fish see colors differently as water and weather conditions change," he says. "So I try different colors until I determine a pattern. As a general rule, I use dark colors on dark days and bright colors on bright days. Translucent colors work anytime. In clear water, whites, grays, chrome and natural colors work best."

Other lure details are important as well, Driscoll says.

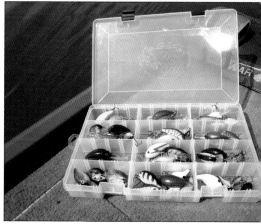

Kent Driscoll with a pair of nice summer crappie caught while trolling crankbaits. His crankbait box contains dozens of colors so he can use the one most appropriate for weather and water conditions.   PHOTOS COURTESY OF Kent Driscoll

"I always use No. 4 Daiichi Bleeding Bait treble hooks," he says. "And I use a swivel to maximize lure action and make lure changes quickly. Red swivels are my 'super secret weapon.'"

Driscoll's trolling system utilizes eight B'n'M Pro Staff Trolling Poles—two each 14-foot, 12-foot, 10-foot and 8-foot—with one of each size on each side of the boat in a 4-foot Driftmaster T-5100 Troll Master trolling bar with four Li'l Pro Series rod holders. Each pole is paired with a Cabela's Depthmaster II line-counter trolling reel spooled with 12-pound Berkley Trilene Big Game line in a high-visibility color.

"The 2-foot rod length differences allow line separation to sweep a larger area and avoid line tangles," Driscoll says. "The line-counter reels are critical for releasing the proper amount of line to determine depth and avoid tangles."

The 14-foot poles are placed in the holders nearest the bow, followed by the 12-foot, 10-foot and 8-foot poles in that order.

The 14-foot poles are pointed perpendicular to the sides of the boat. The crankbaits on these are weighted with a 2-ounce egg sinker 4 feet above the lure and are trolled on 24 feet of line. (No weights are used on any other crankbaits.) The sinker is positioned by running the line through the weight three to four times, which locks it in place like a Carolina rig.

The 12-foot poles also are perpendicular to the boat sides, with lures running on 75 feet of line. The 10-foot poles are angled back 10 degrees with lures on 90 feet of line. Eight-foot poles are angled back 20 degrees with lures on 110 feet of line.

"Your trolling speed should be 1.5 to 2 mph and should be monitored by GPS," says Driscoll. "GPS allows you to mark hotspots and create routes to follow. And it's critical that your unit also has an MMC card so you can follow contours on underwater structure.

"You can catch huge numbers of crappie using this technique because of the large amount of water you cover," he continues. "The more looks your lures get, the more fish you'll catch. In addition, you'll catch the larger, more aggressive fish in each school. Smaller fish are slower and have smaller mouths, making it harder for them to eat a crankbait. Therefore, this is an excellent technique for targeting trophy-class crappie."

Crankin' With Coleman and Capps

When fishing lakes that stratify in summer, Tiptonville, Tennessee, anglers Steve Coleman and Ronnie Capps, the winningest crappie pros in history, get their crappie-catchers into the fish-rich thermocline using a special double-crankbait rig they've refined during years of fishing.

"Structure that crappie typically relate to much of the year becomes uncomfortable to the fish in summer because of lower oxygen levels," says Capps. "These fish move vertically in the water column to find more comfortable conditions and still remain over deep water. They seem to sometimes just 'ride around' in deep water, remaining suspended. This double-crankbait rig fished on multiple poles provides a great way to cover a lot of real estate and find these schools of crappie."

Components of the rig include a Rapala Jointed Shad Rap crankbait (usually Shad or Blue Shad color), a Bandit 200 or 300 Series crankbait (Pearl or Fire Tiger color); two number-6, three-way/inline swivels; a 4- to 6-ounce bank sinker or bass-casting sinker; and four 20-pound-test, P-Line mono leaders (two 30-inch, one 36-inch and one 4-inch).

"We begin by tying the 36-inch leader between the two swivels [to the bottom eye of one swivel and the top eye of the other]," says Coleman. "Then the sinker is connected to the bottom eye of the bottom swivel using the 4-inch leader. Next, we tie a 30-inch leader to each of the crankbaits, and tie each leader to the side eye of one of the swivels. This produces a

Crappie pros Steve Coleman (left) and Ronnie Capps (right) use a specialized double-crankbait trolling technique that has helped them win dozens of summer fishing tournaments around the country.

This simplified view shows the basic configuration of the Capps-Coleman crankbait rig.

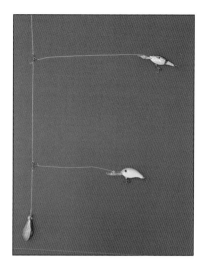

rig with the sinker at the bottom and the two crankbaits on separate lines trailing behind. The main line ties to the top eye of the upper swivel."

"Using the two different styles of crank-baits keeps the lures separate when you're trolling these rigs," Capps says. "The bottom lure, the Bandit crankbait, digs deeper, while the top lure, the Shad Rap, is lighter and stays higher. If you like, you can use a Bandit 100 crankbait on top instead of the Shad Rap. We want the top lure to 'dig and wiggle' and the bottom lure to just wiggle."

The two anglers prefer a trolling speed of 1.5 to 2 miles per hour, "or just fast enough so the ends of the poles vibrate," Coleman says. "The crankbaits produce reaction strikes, and this speed is ideal so the crappie hook themselves when they hit. We usually fish these rigs on four to six 12- or 14-foot B'n'M Pro Staff Trolling Rods set in holders at the front of the boat. This allows us to follow bottom channels and other structure on a GPS when trolling, and with all the poles at the front of the boat, we can make tighter, quicker turns when necessary."

JIM DUCKWORTH AND THE BANDITS

Jim Duckworth of Lebanon, Tennessee, is one of the nation's best-known multi-species anglers. Owner of Ducktrail Guide Service, he's a superb crappie angler and uses crankbaits to catch summer slabs in the Volunteer State lakes he fishes.

The crankbaits Duckworth uses are Bandit Lures' Series 100, 200 and 300. Each of these 2-inch-long baitfish imitations runs at a different depth. The 100s dive 2 to 5 feet, 200s dive 4 to 8 feet and 300s dive 8 to 12 feet.

"My favorite colors, in order of preference, are gray splatter back, chartreuse blue back and silver minnow sparkle," says Duckworth. "I use my fish finder to tell me whether fish are deep or shallow, then I fish the Bandit crankbait that will run just above them."

Duckworth fishes from a 22-foot boat with six poles.

"On the bow, I use two 16-foot B'n'M Slo-Troller rods with Abu Garcia Ambassadeur C3 reels spooled with 20-pound-test Spiderwire Stealth line," he says. "I prefer Stealth because it's strong, and I never lose lures. It also makes the lures vibrate better because it has no stretch, and the line diameter is the same as 8-pound-test so I get good depth. The line on these poles, and all others, is tied to a stainless snap so it's easy to change lures. I place these two rods in Driftmaster rod holders at a 90-degree angle to sides of the boat, and troll the crankbaits on 15 to 30 yards of line.

"In the middle of the boat, 8 feet behind the front rods, I use B'n'M's Jim Duckworth 10-foot Crappie Special rods with Abu Garcia Cardinal 802 reels. These are spooled with 20-pound yellow Stealth line to help me see the lines separately from the front lines. I place these in holders, straight out from the sides of the boat, and with 20 to 40 yards of line from rod tip to lure."

The final two rods are placed 8 feet behind the middle pair. These are 6-foot, medium-action Berkley Lightning Rods paired with C3 reels, with 30 to 50 yards of line from rod to lure. They're angled back 45 degrees to narrow the spread.

"I put one fisherman with two rods," says Duckworth, "then I use my outboard motor to troll the lures at a speed of 2.5 to 3 mph around creek and river channel edges, flats edges and baitfish schools. When I determine the depth and lure color that work best, I switch all rods to the same depth and color and continue that way until the fishing slows. Then I change lures until I find the next good combination."

Duckworth's Bandit crankbait technique works great from postspawn through fall.

"Crappie roam this season, chasing shad until winter," he says. "Trolling crankbaits helps me cover 10-plus miles a day so I can find the sweet spots where they are feeding."

Trolling Bandit crankbaits on multiple poles is the ticket for summer crappie-fishing success for Tennessee guide Jim Duckworth. PHOTO COURTESY OF Tim Huffman

TROPHY TACTICS

ONE GUIDE'S SECRETS FOR GIANT CRAPPIE

An angler who consistently catches crappie must possess many positive attributes. He must have an in-depth knowledge of crappie behavior. He must know where crappie are likely to be found throughout the seasons and under a wide variety of weather and water conditions. He must know the best baits and lures for enticing his quarry in each body of water he fishes and the right ways to present those enticements so crappie want to eat them.

When your *vocation* is crappie fishing, it's even more important to be in tune with the ways of these popular panfish. In addition, you must be able to quickly adapt to changing or unfamiliar conditions. Because your livelihood depends on your ability to put fish in the boat, you need enough tricks up your sleeve to make this happen even under the worse circumstances. In other words, you need to be flexible and innovative—ready to try something new or different when "regular" fishing tactics won't produce.

This latter group of anglers includes tournament pros and fishing guides, and in a few rare instances, people like Todd Huckabee of Eufaula, Oklahoma, who make their living doing both. I've been fortunate to fish with several such individuals, but I can say without reservation, none comes close to Huckabee when it comes to flexibility and innovation. This crappie expert is always thinking "outside the box"

Oklahoma crappie guide and tournament pro Todd Huckabee uses innovative tactics to put trophy crappie like this in the boat.
PHOTO COURTESY OF Lawrence Taylor, PRADCO Fishing

and has developed several slab-hooking techniques that are out of the ordinary, yet astoundingly productive, for heavyweight fish.

Huckabee spends an average of 270 days annually fishing for crappie. As a full-time crappie guide, he fishes with clients on several Oklahoma lakes about 150 days each year. He also is a respected tournament professional, having qualified often for events like the Crappie USA Classic and CAST (Crappie Angler Sportsman Tour) Classic.

Few anglers are more qualified to give advice on catching big slabs and lots of them. And Huckabee kindly agreed to share some of his secrets for waylaying out-sized crappie. The tips that follow could help you catch some of the biggest crappie you've ever seen.

Facts About Shad, Brush Piles and Big Crappie

On a March day several years ago, Huckabee invited me to join him for a crappie fishing trip on Oklahoma's Eufaula Lake, a 102,000-acre Corps of Engineers impoundment 12 miles east of Eufaula.

"We have two basic choices," he said when I arrived. "We can try to catch a lot of crappie, or we can focus on catching trophy-size crappie."

I chose the latter, figuring Huckabee would head for some hidden brush piles or other fish attractors like most guides with whom I've fished. To my surprise, that was not the case.

Huckabee explained that in Eufaula Lake and other waters with abundant schools of threadfin shad, big crappie are more likely to be found near schools of shad than holding around brush piles. Unlike small crappie, which find a safe haven from predators in a brush pile's maze of branches, these 2-pound-plus giants aren't on the menu of many meat-eaters. Their own appetite is substantial, however, so they follow roaming shad schools, feasting on these high-protein baitfish to fuel their internal furnaces.

"Lots of brush piles placed in an area may actually keep big crappie away," said Huckabee. "The schools of shad these big crappie feed on prefer open waters without obstructions that block their movements. If brush piles are in the area, the fish must go around them. They don't like this, so they avoid these areas. You'll catch more and bigger crappie if you fish near underwater ledges, riprapped banks or even the bottom where shad are schooling."

Huckabee flipped on his fish finder and showed me a compact band of pixels running across the screen that indicated a big school of threadfins 10 feet below the boat. Crappie appeared as scattered blips around and beneath the shad. Find this signature, Huckabee said, and you can target the crappie with lures appropriate to the situation.

Tackle Tips

"Big crappie feeding on big baitfish often ignore the 1/64- to 1/16-ounce jigs many crappie anglers use," Huckabee told me. "Trophy-class crappie like to fill their bellies with one big bite, not several little ones, so I use lures much larger than those other fishermen typically tie on."

The lures in this case were 2-inch Yum Wooly Beavertails on 1/8-ounce Lindy X-Change jigheads. Huckabee pinched off the head of each soft-plastic lure, then rigged two on each line about 18 inches apart, each on a dropper loop.

"If shad are 8 to 10 feet deep," he said, "position the jigs so they'll be at 8 to 10 feet during a slow troll. Maintain a boat speed that keeps your line perpendicular to the water's surface. Slightly lift and drop the rig as you move, maintaining a feel of the bottom as the weight bumps along."

As we fished Eufaula Lake, Huckabee kept his eyes on the sonar, and we kept our Beavertail rigs working in and around the shad schools. Whenever we reached the edge of a school, Huckabee turned the boat and trolled through the school again. Typically, we caught two or more crappie on each pass. All these were true trophy-class fish. During four hours working open-water shad schools, I caught seventeen crappie. The smallest weighed 2 pounds, 1 ounce. The rest were slightly larger.

Crankbait Crappie

Keeping with Huckabee's "bigger is better" lure theme, you might try a big crankbait to entice deep summer slabs. Huckabee inno-vated a technique that employs a Rebel Crappie Crank-R crankbait to catch 2-pound-plus crappie.

"When big crappie go deep in winter, their metabolism stays pretty high," he said. "These fish are preparing for the spawn, and they're eating a lot. But during summer, these same deep-water

Larger-than-normal lures like Yum Wooly Beavertails are standard crappie-catchers for Todd Huckabee. PHOTO COURTESY OF Lawrence Taylor, PRADCO Fishing

Big crankbaits like Rebel's Crappie Crank-R look like bass enticements but often prove irresistible to barn-door crappie as well.

crappie are kind of lazy. If you drop a lure like a Beavertail down to them, often it's just not enough to entice them. They really don't seem interested in eating something unless it's bigger. That's why I use crankbaits.

"You make this rig with a 1/8- to 1/4-ounce tungsten weight above a barrel swivel on the main line," Huckabee continued. "Then tie a 3- to 4-foot leader from the swivel to the crankbait. Cast it out, let it sink, then just crawl the lure across the bottom. Big crappie that won't dart out after smaller prey find it hard to resist a big meal like this."

Huckabee likes to further modify the Crappie Crank-R in a way that also can be used on other crankbaits, like Bomber's Fat Free Fry or Fat Free Shad.

"I modify each lure by removing the back treble hook and placing a crappie tube skirt on the hook's shank," said Huckabee. "The hook is then replaced. The skirt works just like the feathers on some topwater plugs, giving the lure more action. I like to alternate colors of the components. For example, I might use a crankbait that has a citrus-shad color and add a pink skirt. This seems more effective than using components with similar colors."

Huckabee uses this rig to target crappie when they're feeding on threadfin shad around shoreline riprap and rocks.

"The shad often are right up on the rocks where you can see them," he says. "The crappie position themselves beneath the baitfish, usually in 5 or 6 feet of water. I fish the Crappie Crank-Rs just like I might fish them for bass—working them parallel to the bank, cranking them down to the rocks and making contact with the bottom. Then I slow the lure down and just wait for a big crappie to strike."

During a typical year Huckabee may catch more than 200 crappie, each exceeding 2 pounds, using these rigs.

Shallow Summer Crappie

During the blistering 100-degree days often seen in late summer, most anglers seek crappie in deep-water haunts. Once again, Huckabee breaks the mold.

"I've learned to look for big crappie up on shallow flats [1 to 3 feet deep] in creeks this time of year," he said. "Shad spawn over and over again in these areas, as

The Yum Dinger doesn't resemble anything a crappie would eat, but it's proven effective for catching summer crappie in the shallows.

long as conditions are right. And the big crappie follow them. The crappie are always next to some piece of cover such as a laydown, a log jam or a standing stump. And flats where cover is sparse are best because, on these, any little stick will hold fish. The water needs to be stained."

Huckabee discovered trophy crappie in these locales while bass fishing and decided to experiment with different fishing techniques until he found one that worked best.

"The best lure in this situation seems to be a 2-inch, black/pink Yum Wooly Beavertail on a Lindy X-Change jig head," he said. "And I found the crappie tend to hold near one particular kind of cover each day. One day they may be on laydowns, and I catch more if I work that cover. The next day they may be on log jams or stumps, and working the Beavertail around that cover is more productive."

Huckabee also targets big summer crappie in flooded willows. Here again, the rig he uses is somewhat different from the norm.

"I catch a ton of postspawn crappie by wacky-rigging a 3-inch Yum Dinger and fishing it around water willows and around shallow brush close to docks. They can't resist the slow fall and wiggle of a Dinger that's rigged this way with the hook run through the center of the lure. The 4-inch Dingers work, too, but I found I get a better hooking ratio with the smaller lure. This is a fun way to fish because of the numbers of other crappie you catch."

Shallow Winter Crappie

Most anglers also think crappie return to deep water in winter. But, "For years, I have caught limits of big winter crappie in water less than 10 feet, fishing 1 to 3 feet deep," says Huckabee.

He does this by fishing at night around a crappie light dropped beside or within a boat dock.

"Any dock that has brush and at least 10 feet of water will hold crappie," he says. "The crappie light attracts freshwater shrimp, which in turn attract ghost minnows and shad. Crappie move in to eat these baitfish and usually suspend just below the Styrofoam under the docks."

Huckabee uses a tandem rig—two Lindy X-Change jigs, 1/16-ounce on top and 1/8-ounce on bottom—and starts by fishing around 3 feet deep. He then works down in the water column in increments of 2 feet until he finds crappie.

"On clear lakes, if the action is hot and then dies, turn off your light and the crappie will start biting again," he says. "Do not leave your light off for long, ten to fifteen minutes maximum, or your ecosystem will fall apart.

"The main key is persistence," he continues. "Some nights are great, and some are slow. The great nights are truly unbelievable."

And unbelievably, Huckabee is catching these fish in shallow water beneath a crappie light on nights that are incredibly cold. Fishing this way is usually done on hot summer nights over deep cover and structure.

More Innovations

It seems like every time I talk with Todd, he's come up with another new tactic that's dynamite on giant crappie. His bag of tricks runs deep already, but he's continually studying crappie behavior and experimenting with new lures and new ways of fishing that will give him an edge on tournament competitors and make him a better guide.

If you, too, want to be a better crappie angler, I suggest you follow his lead. Don't get stuck in a rut. Think outside the box occasionally. Innovation often leads to success.

Few anglers look for winter crappie in less than 10 feet of water, but Todd Huckabee often nabs cold-water fish in shallow water beneath boat docks.

DIPPIN' CRAPPIE

According to Oklahoma crappie guide Todd Huckabee, on some crappie lakes, there's a saying among tournament anglers: "The guy that dips the most trees wins."

Dippin' is a way of fishing standing timber in water as deep as 20 feet.

"This tactic works best in areas with 'slick' timber," Huckabee says. "By that, I mean timber that's pretty much just like a telephone pole. I believe bigger crappie like this better because they can move around it

better. Crappie a pound or less prefer to have some branches or brush, but the larger crappie don't."

The lure Huckabee uses for dippin' is a Yum Wooly Beavertail or Yum Wooly Zapper on a 3/16-ounce jighead.

"I drop the lure next to the timber and either catch a fish or move on to the next pole," Huckabee says. "The secret is to let the lure sit for ten seconds to a minute before ever moving it. If you don't have a bite by then, move the lure up very slowly in a controlled fashion. Fish it slowly all the way around the pole, then move to the next pole."

Huckabee says dippin' works year-round except during the spawn or during real high water.

"You may have to come back and fish around the same pole five times before a fish will hit," he notes. "I think the crappie sometimes leave their pole to go feed, then return to rest. And after you finally catch one, there may not be another fish on the same pole that day."

"Bigger baits, slick structure and repeated offerings": those are keys for dippin' slabs, says Huckabee.

TIPS FOR CATCHING SLABS

How can you catch your biggest crappie ever? Many anglers want a simple answer to that question—a magic pill, a silver bullet, some tight-lipped secret the anglers who are consistently catching trophy crappie must know about but won't tell.

Unfortunately, there's not one. But there are proven tactics you can employ that are likely to add up to eventual success. Here are some to get you started.

Fish the Best Waters

All waters are not created equal. You'll home in on a trophy quicker if you choose those proven to produce extra-large crappie, even if it means traveling. Contact your state fisheries department or a local fisheries biologist for information that will lead to such waters. Check with agencies in other states, too, and if necessary, plan a vacation that will take you to some of the best waters.

Some lakes and reservoirs have special management regulations such as length or slot limits that encourage the growth of larger crappie. These, in particular, are worth trying.

Avoid Crowds

Barn-door crappie get cagey when people and boats are swarming. Fish when fewer folks are on the water—weekdays, in winter, at night. Better yet, fish fertile back-

Slab crappie aren't available everywhere. If you're hoping to catch a trophy, fish lakes known to produce heavyweights.

country crappie waters that seldom see other anglers. These often are found in wildlife management areas, national wildlife refuges and national forests. Many of them hold gigantic crappie, thanks to the lack of fishing pressure.

Watch for Isolated Underwater Cover

Larger crappie often use isolated underwater logs, treetops, etc., instead of visible cover pounded by more anglers. The hotspots usually are near (not necessarily in) deeper water, where big crappie can simply move deeper when feeling threatened.

The Northwest Factor

During prespawn periods, you'll have an advantage if you fish a lake's northwest section. Cold northerly winds blow over northwest banks, resulting in water that's as much as 5 degrees warmer here. This is highly attractive to big prespawn slabs.

Fish Often, Year-round

Spawning season offers the best slab-hooking opportunities. Crappie move shallow then and are more easily found. Big egg-laden females weigh more than after spawning. However, savvy trophy hunters know big crappie can be taken year-round, and those who take trophy fish consistently are on the water many days year-round. Follow their example. Don't wait for perfect conditions. Get out there and fish.

Don't Blow a Chance

Don't lose the crappie of a lifetime because of avoidable problems: the line was frayed or too light for conditions, the hooks didn't hold, the drag was too loose or too tight or the tackle was inadequate. Check often for fraying; cut and retie if necessary. Use the heaviest line suitable for conditions. Use premium hooks, always needle-sharp. Always set your drag properly. Use quality poles, rods, reels and other tackle.

Fishing year-round improves an angler's chances of boating barn-door crappie like this.

Be Different

Are other anglers zigging? Maybe you should zag. Fish become conditioned to certain baits, lures and presentations, and you may catch more lunkers by trying something unconventional—a rosy red minnow instead of a golden shiner, for example, or a new lure or presentation that hasn't caught on yet. Be open-minded. Experiment.

Try Crankbaits

Although you may not catch as many fish, crappie taken on crankbaits average larger than fish taken on jigs or minnows. Also, because crankbaits are a little heavier than most other crappie baits, they can be cast farther with light tackle. This allows you to keep well away from the area you're fishing, a real advantage when targeting usually spooky trophies.

Big crankbaits often entice big crappie.

Play It Right

Crappie are called "papermouths" with good reason. It's easy to tear the hook from the mouth if you apply too much pressure. But you can lose a big crappie just as easily by applying too little pressure. Keep a tight line at all times, but don't play the fish too long or too hard.

Move off Small Crappie

Small crappie are good practice subjects, but if you start catching lots of runts when targeting slabs, move somewhere else. The little guys are fun, but big ones aren't likely to be among them.

Try Shallower Water

In the situation just mentioned, most anglers will tend to move deeper. Deep water holds mystique; we believe it's where the lunkers lurk. But that's not the case with crappie in most waters. When catching loads of small crappie, more often than not you'll find Mr. Big in shallower water, not deeper. Try it and see.

They don't call them "papermouths" for nothing. Using a landing net helps assure you won't lose that special trophy crappie.

Don't Forget Hotspots

Remember the precise locations where you catch, lose or see big crappie—the specific stump, the particular bush, etc. A return visit could turn up the barn door you missed, another trophy that moved in or a crappie that grew bigger after you released it. Use a good lake map or, better yet, a GPS unit, to mark hotspots in case memory fails.

Always Use a Landing Net

Bad things happen when you don't use a net: the fish thrashes off when you bend to grab it, or the hook rips out when you try swinging it in. A landing net is the best way to efficiently handle big crappie. Use one with a long handle that lets you stand while netting, giving an extra few feet of reach when you need it most.

CLEANING AND COOKING CRAPPIE

HOW TO PAN-DRESS AND FILLET CRAPPIE

After the fun and excitement of crappie fishing has subsided, anglers must clean their catch. Two basic ways—filleting and pan-dressing, both of which are illustrated in this chapter—are used to prepare crappie for the table. Tools you need include a sharp fillet knife; a cutting board, fillet board or other hard, flat surface (use plastic or glass to reduce bacteria); a spoon or scaling tool, if you're pan-dressing the fish; and some newspaper or a bucket for disposal of waste parts. Also recommended is household bleach for clean-up.

When properly cared for and prepared, crappie are among the most delectable of all freshwater fishes.   PHOTO BY Jack Bissell

After the fish are cleaned, they can be cooked and eaten, or you can store the fillets or pan-dressed fish in the freezer until you're ready to prepare them. To avoid freezer burn and preserve freshness, it's best to immerse the prepared fish in water when you freeze them (either in zip-seal plastic freezer bags or plastic containers) or better yet, to vacuum-seal them using a product such as the Tilia FoodSaver. Be careful the sharp fins on pan-dressed fish aren't positioned in such a way they could puncture the wrapping or container. Use frozen fish within six months for the best flavor.

How to Pan-Dress a Crappie

To pan-dress a crappie, you simply scrape away all the scales with a spoon or scaling tool, cut off the fish's head, remove the entrails, wash the fish thoroughly inside and out and *voila*, you're finished. Leave the fins, tail and skin on. These are delicious in

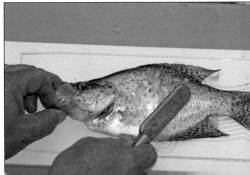

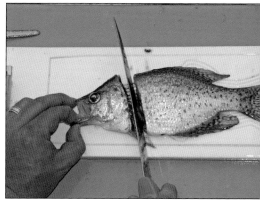

their own special ways and enhance the unsurpassed flavor of these popular panfish. You'll have to separate meat and bone as you eat pan-dressed fish, but many crappie connoisseurs believe this method of preparation produces a tastier result.

How to Fillet a Crappie

Filleting is a popular way to prepare crappie for cooking. Simply cut the flesh away from the bones and skin. The result is a boneless piece of fish ready to be cooked. You need a sharp fillet knife with a long, thin, flexible blade and a smooth cutting surface.

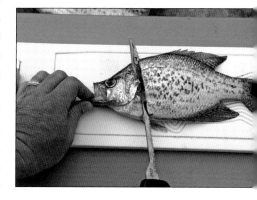

1. Lay the fish on a cutting board or other flat, hard surface. Grasping the fish's mouth, take the fillet knife and position it just behind the side (pectoral) fin. Slice downward to the backbone, keeping the rear of the knife blade up. Be careful not to cut into the fish's backbone.

2. Turn the knife blade toward the tail and continue cutting, staying on top of the back and belly fins. You'll feel resistance as you cut through the rib cage, but be careful not to cut into the backbone. It's better to cut too shallow than too deep. Continue your cut toward the tail, until you have almost, but not quite, cut the scaly fillet off.

3. With the fillet barely attached to the tail, flip it away from the fish. Position your knife on the narrow portion of the fillet, and while holding the fish, slice between the meat and the skin to remove the fillet. To obtain the maximum meat, cut very close to the skin. When the fillet is removed, place it, with rib cage still attached, on a sheet of wax paper. Flip the fish over and fillet the other side.

4. To finish, take each fillet, and with the tip of your fillet knife, carefully cut out the rib cage. To retrieve the most meat, angle your knife and slice close to the ribs. After you rinse the fillets, they're ready to cook or store.

CLEANING AND FREEZING TIPS

- Beware of the sharp, spiny fins when cleaning crappie. They can cause nasty puncture wounds.

Always cut away from you when filleting a fish. If the knife slips, it's less likely to cut you.

- An ordinary office clipboard fastened to your cleaning table makes the job of cleaning crappie much easier. The clip will hold the tail or head firmly while you scale or fillet your catch.
- To keep crappie scales from flying all over when cleaning your catch, scale the fish underwater in a dishpan or sink.
- The waste created from cleaning fish can get smelly if you clean your fish on Saturday and your garbage pickup is on Tuesday. Wrap the waste in newspaper and tape it securely, then store in your freezer until garbage day to reduce offensive odors.
- You can extend freezer life of fish by several months if you soak the fish for twenty seconds in lemon juice. The ascorbic acid in lemon juice retards spoilage by slowing the growth of microorganisms and counteracting oxidation.

CRAPPIE RECIPES

The delicate white flesh of the crappie is delicious and easy to prepare. With many cooks, it's often into the frying pan, onto the platter, don't spare the salt and pepper, and please pass the ketchup. Even so, one of the crappie's greatest assets is its versatility. Serve it fried, smoked, poached, baked, broiled, braised, sautéed or barbecued. Or combine it with other foods for casseroles, chowders or other favorites. Crappie can be eaten in a sandwich, in a salad, on a pizza or in an omelet. You're limited only by your imagination.

The most important rule when preparing crappie is never overcook it. Crappie is naturally tender and cooks quickly. It's done when it flakes easily when tested with a fork. Cook it too long, and it becomes dry and tough. Remember, too, the shorter the time from hook to cook, the better the flavor.

The following recipes offer a variety of ways to add the delectable flavor of crappie to your menus.

Fried Crappie, Arkansas Style

Fried Crappie,
Arkansas Style

2 pounds crappie fillets or pan-dressed fish
1 (3-oz.) bottle Louisiana hot sauce
4 cups milk
3/4 cup yellow cornmeal
1/4 cup flour
2 teaspoons salt
1/2 teaspoon cayenne pepper
1/2 teaspoon garlic powder
Peanut oil

Marinate the fish 1 hour in a large bowl in which the hot sauce and milk have been mixed. Remove the fish and drain. Combine the dry ingredients by shaking them together in a large plastic bag. Add the fish and shake to coat. Add peanut oil to a cooker or skillet and heat to 365 degrees. Add fish pieces in a single layer, and fry until fish flakes easily with a fork, about 5 to 6 minutes. Remove and drain on paper towels. Repeat with remaining fish. Makes six to eight servings.

Beer-Batter Crappie

    Vegetable or peanut oil for frying

    8 crappie fillets or pan-dressed fish

    Salt, pepper to taste

    1 cup all-purpose flour

    2 tablespoons garlic powder

    2 tablespoons paprika

    2 teaspoons salt

    2 teaspoons freshly ground black pepper

    1 egg, beaten

    1 (12-oz.) can or bottle beer

Heat the oil in a deep fryer to 365 degrees. Rinse fish fillets, pat dry and season with salt and pepper.

Combine flour, garlic powder, paprika, salt and pepper. Stir the egg into these dry ingredients. Gradually mix in beer until a thin batter is formed. You should be able to see the fish through the batter after it has been dipped.

Dip fish fillets into the batter, and then drop one at a time into the hot oil. Fry, turning once, until both sides are golden brown and fish flakes easily with a fork. Drain on paper towels, and serve warm. Makes four servings.

Crappie Po'boys

    6 large crusty rolls

    1 cup ketchup

    3 dashes Tabasco sauce

    1 tablespoon prepared mustard

    1 tablespoon minced onion

    6 fried crappie fillets (12 if they're small)

    Dill pickles

    Shredded lettuce

Cut the rolls in half, lengthwise, scoop out the soft centers and place in the oven until hot but not crispy. Combine ketchup, Tabasco, mustard and onion. Spread this mixture on a hot roll, and then top with a crappie fillet (two if they're small), dill pickles, lettuce and the top of the roll. Makes six servings.

Crappie Po'boy

Onion-Dijon Crusted Crappie Fillets

1 onion, finely chopped

1/4 cup honey Dijon mustard

8 to 12 crappie fillets

Garlic salt, pepper to taste

Dried parsley flakes

Preheat your oven to 350 degrees. In a small bowl, mix together the onion and mustard. Season the crappie fillets with garlic salt and pepper. Place on a baking tray and coat with the onion/mustard mixture. Sprinkle parsley flakes over the top. Bake for 15 minutes in the preheated oven, then turn the oven to broil. Broil until golden, 3 to 5 minutes. Makes four to six servings.

Creole Crappie

1 pound crappie fillets, cut in bite-sized pieces

1 (16-oz.) can stewed tomatoes, with liquid

2 teaspoons dried minced onion

1 teaspoon chicken bouillon granules

1/2 teaspoon dried oregano

1/4 teaspoon garlic powder

1/8 teaspoon hot pepper sauce

Cooked rice

In a medium saucepan, combine the tomatoes (with juices), dried onion, bouillon granules, dried oregano, garlic powder and hot pepper sauce; bring to a boil and stir in the crappie pieces. Cover and cook over medium heat for 5 to 8 minutes or until the fish flakes easily when tested with a fork and is opaque all the way through. Serve over the rice. Makes four to six servings.

Microwave Manhattan-Style Crappie Chowder

1/2 cup chopped green onions

1/4 cup chicken broth

1 pound crappie fillets, cut in bite-sized pieces

1 (24-oz.) can vegetable juice cocktail

1 (12-oz.) can whole kernel corn with sweet red peppers, drained

Microwave Manhattan-Style
Crappie Chowder

1 teaspoon Worcestershire sauce

1/8 teaspoon hot pepper sauce

In a 2-quart microwave-safe dish, combine green onion and chicken broth. Cover and microwave on high for 2 minutes or until onion is tender.

Add remaining ingredients, cover, and cook on high for 8 to 10 minutes or until fish flakes with a fork and chowder is heated through. Stir twice while cooking. Makes four to six servings.

Scrumptious Parmesan Crappie

1-1/2 to 2 pounds crappie fillets

1 (12-oz.) can evaporated milk

1-1/2 cups all-purpose flour

1/2 cup grated Parmesan cheese

1 tablespoon Italian seasoning

2 teaspoons baking powder

1 tablespoon garlic powder

1 tablespoon ground dry mustard

1 tablespoon onion powder

1 teaspoon salt

1 teaspoon fresh-ground black pepper

1 cup melted butter

Pat the crappie fillets dry with paper towels, place in a shallow dish and pour the evaporated milk over them. Cover and refrigerate for six hours or overnight.

Preheat the oven to 400 degrees. In a large mixing bowl, combine flour, cheese, Italian seasoning, baking powder, garlic powder, dry mustard, onion powder, salt and pepper. Remove the fish fillets from the milk and dredge in the flour mixture.

Spray a rimmed baking sheet with non-stick cooking spray like PAM and place the coated fillets on the pan. Drizzle melted butter over the fish. Bake 15 to 20 minutes, or until the fish flakes easily when tested with a fork. Makes three to four servings.

Down-South Crappie Cakes

Instant mashed potato granules

1 pound crappie fillets, finely chopped

2 teaspoons grated onion

1/2 teaspoon salt

1/2 teaspoon Louisiana hot sauce

1 egg, beaten

1/3 cup dried bread crumbs

Down-South Crappie Cakes

1 tablespoon vegetable oil

1 tablespoon butter or margarine

About 1 hour before serving, prepare instant mashed potato granules as label directs for 1 cup mashed potatoes (or use 1 cup leftover mashed potatoes). Cover and refrigerate thirty minutes.

In a medium bowl, stir chopped fish, onion, salt, hot sauce and mashed potatoes until blended. With your hands, shape the fish mixture into four 3-inch round cakes.

Place the beaten egg in a pie plate, and the bread crumbs on a sheet of waxed paper. Dip the fish cakes into the egg, then dredge in bread crumbs.

Heat the vegetable oil and butter in a skillet, and cook the fish cakes until browned on both sides and fish is done, about 8 minutes. Arrange fish cakes on warm platter, and garnish with tartar sauce, lemon wedges and parsley sprigs. Makes four servings.

Crappie and Scallops Casserole

3 tablespoons butter or margarine

1/2 cup diced green pepper

1/2 cup diced onion

1/4 cup diced celery

1/2 pound crappie fillets

1/2 pound scallops

1 (5-oz.) can evaporated milk

1 (10-3/4-oz.) can condensed cream of shrimp soup

1/4 pound cooked peeled shrimp

1 (4-oz.) jar diced pimentos

1/2 teaspoon white pepper

1 teaspoon seasoned salt

Heat butter in a skillet and sauté pepper, onion and celery until tender. Cut fish in bite-sized pieces, and place on top of the onion mixture. Cover and simmer about 5 minutes. Cut each scallop into two or three pieces. Add to the pan and cook five minutes more. Add the evaporated milk, cream of shrimp soup, shrimp, pimentos and seasonings. Pour into a greased casserole. Cool, cover and refrigerate overnight. Add a few pats of butter to the top. Bake 30 to 40 minutes in a preheated 350-degree oven. Makes four to six servings.

Crappie With Lemon, Butter and Herbs

1 tablespoon butter

1 pound crappie fillets

Crappie With Lemon, Butter and Herbs

1 lemon

1 teaspoon each chopped parsley, chives and rosemary

Melt the butter and pour into a shallow baking dish. Arrange the crappie fillets in the dish. Cut the lemon in half, and squeeze about 1 tablespoon of lemon juice over the fillets. Sprinkle with the herbs. Slice the remaining lemon half into thin slices, and arrange the slices on top of the fish. Bake in a preheated 450-degree oven for 12 minutes or until fish flakes easily with a fork. Makes two to four servings.

Deep-Fried Crappie with Crawfish Sauce

2 pounds crappie fillets or pan-dressed fish

1 cup yellow cornmeal

1/2 cup flour

1 tablespoon salt

1 teaspoon fresh-ground black pepper

1/2 cup butter, divided

1/4 cup chopped onion

1/4 cup chopped celery

1/4 cup chopped bell pepper

1 tablespoon minced garlic

2 tablespoons dry white wine

1 pound peeled crawfish tails

1/4 cup sliced green onions

1/4 cup whipping cream

1/4 cup fresh sliced mushrooms

Dash hot pepper sauce

Dredge the crappie pieces in a mixture of the cornmeal, flour, salt and pepper. Deep fry in oil heated to 365 degrees. Set aside on paper towels to drain. Keep warm.

To prepare the Crawfish Sauce, melt half of the butter in a heavy sauté pan over medium-high heat. Add chopped onion, celery, bell pepper and garlic. Cook until vegetables are wilted, about three to five minutes. Stir in wine, and then add crawfish, green onion and mushrooms. Cook about five minutes or until crawfish are hot and wine is slightly reduced. Stir in cream and hot pepper sauce and cook six to eight minutes or until cream is reduced and thickened. Remove from heat. Cut remaining 1/4 cup butter into pieces and add a few pieces at a time stirring constantly. Adjust seasoning and serve over fried crappie. Makes four to six servings.

Crappie Ceviche

1 cup lemon juice

1 cup lime juice

1 pound crappie fillets, diced in 1/8-inch cubes

1/2 cup chopped fresh cilantro leaves

2 tomatoes, quartered, seeded, cut in small strips

1 small purple onion, chopped

1 jalapeño pepper, finely diced

Mix the lemon and lime juices in a large bowl. Reserve half for the final preparation. Combine the remaining half with the diced crappie in a non-metallic bowl. Cover and refrigerate overnight.

The next day, combine the cilantro, tomato, onion and jalapeño pepper in a mixing bowl. Stir in the crappie after straining it and discarding all the marinating juices. Stir in the remaining 1 cup of lemon/lime juice.

Crappie Ceviche

Arrange the ceviche in four equal portions in bowls or on salad plates. Garnish with citrus fruit slices. Serve with crackers or tortilla chips. Makes four servings.

Campfire Crappie with Hot Melted Butter

2 pounds crappie fillets or pan-dressed fish

Non-stick cooking spray

1 cup butter

2 teaspoons Worcestershire sauce

2 teaspoons prepared mustard

2 tablespoons chili sauce

2 drops Tabasco sauce

4 teaspoons lemon juice

2 tablespoons chopped parsley

Place crappie on squares of heavy-duty aluminum foil sprayed with non-stick cooking spray. Cook in campfire coals or on the grill ten minutes or until fish flakes easily with a fork.

Melt butter in a saucepan, and add remaining ingredients. Heat until bubbly. Serve over cooked fish. Makes four to six servings.

Crappie Scampi

1 stick butter, melted

2 tablespoons extra-virgin olive oil

10 crappie fillets

2 tablespoons minced garlic

1 teaspoon oregano

Salt, pepper to taste

1/4 cup Italian bread crumbs

1/2 lemon

Pour the melted butter and olive oil over the bottom of a large glass baking dish. Top with the crappie fillets. Season with garlic, oregano, salt and pepper. Cook in a preheated 350-degree oven for fifteen to twenty minutes. Remove from the oven and sprinkle the seasoned bread crumbs over the fillets. Return to the oven and cook an additional five minutes. Makes five servings.

INDEX